To Do What the Day Demands

To Do What the Day Demands

The Life of Father Kaspar Stanggassinger

OTTO WEISS

Translated from the second corrected German edition by Tony Kiesenhofer

Edited by Paul Laverdure and a team of Redemptorists

Liguori
LIGUORI, MISSOURI

Imprimi Potest:
Harry Grile, CSsR, Provincial
Denver Province, The Redemptorists

Published by Liguori Publications
Liguori, Missouri 63057
To order, call 800-325-9521, or visit liguori.org

Library of Congress Cataloging-in-Publication Data

Weiss, Otto, 1934-

To do what the day demands : the life of Father Kaspar Stanggassinger / Otto Weiss ; translated from the second corrected German edition by Tony Kiesenhofer ; edited by Paul Laverdure and a team of Redemptorists.—1st ed.

p. cm.

Includes bibliographical references.

ISBN 978-0-7648-2071-7

1. Stanggassinger, Kaspar, 1871–1899. 2. Blessed—Germany—Biography. I. Laverdure, Paul. II. Title.

BX4705.S794W45 2011

282.092—dc22

[B]

2011012757

Liguori Publications, a nonprofit corporation, is an apostolate of the Redemptorists. To learn more about the Redemptorists, visit Redemptorists.com.

Printed in the United States of America

15 14 13 12 11 / 5 4 3 2 1

First Edition

CONTENTS

INTRODUCTION

Father Kaspar Stanggassinger died on September 26, 1899, before he reached the age of 29. He had done his duty. He was a beloved educator. He did not accomplish anything extraordinary. After his death, when some of his colleagues started to gather information about his life, Father Kaspar Stamm, who was held in high esteem by the Bavarian Redemptorists, exclaimed, "Why all the ruckus? He was a good, young priest."[1] Therefore, his burial was not any different from that of others at the monastery at Gars on the Inn River. Since he had been transferred there just a few weeks before his death, the local population barely noticed his death. Walking behind his casket were only his relatives, his Redemptorist confreres, his students, and a few diocesan priests from Munich.[2]

Unusual, however, was that even decades later, he was not forgotten, neither among the Redemptorists nor among so many others. His biography was published only three years after his death, and a short time later this biography saw a second edition. As was the custom at the death of a Redemptorist, the chronicler of the Gars residence had asked relatives and friends for details about the deceased. Soon he received more material than he could handle. But it was not the massive amount of material, but the contents of the various reports from Stanggassinger's friends and acquaintances that led the chronicler to give the biography a wider audience.[3]

After that, Father Stanggassinger's reputation spread remarkably. More than just a few who were close to him considered him a saint during his lifetime. Now many turned to him in prayer and believed they were miraculously heard.[4] In April 1935, his beatification process was formally begun. At the same time a healing occurred that was believed to be based on his intercession. The doctors testified, "Here a higher power has intervened."[5]

Despite the fact that the reputation of his holiness has spread far beyond Austria's borders to Brazil and California, Africa and India,[6] he himself never traveled to exotic locations. Of course, many who seek his intercession assert, "He is a saint, but he is a human saint; not someone who has left the earth behind, but a human being like you and me who, day-in and day-out, did not do anything else but what each of us do." How he did it was different. It is exactly this difference that makes his holiness so attractive.

ENDNOTES*

1 Zeunisse 208.
2 Causa Mon. 144, 148, 165, 357, 382.
3 *Meier*, Foreword to the first edition.
4 Causa Mon. 267, 271, 331, 339, 364, 379; Suppl. 24, 36, 61.
5 Summarium 316–48; Relazione sulla seduta della C.M. della S.C.
6 Schuster–Wildenauer 157.

* **NOTE: Explanations of endnotes and abbreviations start on page 165.**

CHAPTER ONE

CHILDHOOD AND YOUTH

"A priest, this is what I want to become one day."

KASPAR STANGGASSINGER AT THE AGE OF TWO AND A HALF

Kaspar Stanggassinger's life began in Berchtesgaden. He was born on January 12, 1871, in the mountains in one of the most beautiful corners of Bavaria. He was the second of sixteen children. His father, also named Kaspar, was a well-to-do man. He was a farmer in Unterkälberstein, the owner of a rock quarry and a shipping business. He also held a position in both local and provincial government, and today we would say today that his word carried considerable weight. People used to say that his son, Kaspar, inherited "a tireless power to create" and also "a clear-headed outlook on life."[1]

As was customary, his father engaged in local politics at a tavern table—something that did not set well with Kaspar's mother. Family members clearly remembered that on this very point young Kaspar once had a serious talk with his father when they were together setting up the yearly Nativity scene.[2] Later, when he was a novice with the Redemptorists, he wrote to his father never to forget to bring God into his public life and his daily work.[3]

Kreszenz, his mother, was a good and pious person, with more of a serious disposition. While she experienced much joy in caring for her large family, she likewise had to deal with many difficulties. To her children she passed on a sense of sincerity and piety. Kaspar showed both of these qualities early in his youth, and they matured as he grew older. During the process of his beatification more than thirty years after his death, a number of witnesses could remark, "He got this from his mother." He himself said of his mother, "From my childhood onward, she led me to God." This, he thought, was the beginning of his Christian life and set him in the right direction.[4]

Kaspar also had an especially close relationship with his maternal grandmother. She, too, was a good and even saintly woman. She proved indispensable in helping her daughter in the home. Whenever she changed Kaspar's diapers, she prayed that God might lead Kaspar to the priesthood. At an advanced age, she began to have doubts whether she had acted well in her life. However, her grandson, now away at the seminary, comforted her. He wrote to her that God's grace knows no boundaries. He wished that she would live to see his ordination. But this was not to be. When the news of her death reached him right after his reception of what, in those days, were called "minor orders," he could not hold back his tears. Still, he found words to comfort his parents: "She was happy in her hour of death. She reached all her goals and finished her journey. She is now in heaven."[5]

In his relationships with his siblings, Kaspar was especially close to Elizabeth, almost two years his senior,[6] and to his sister, Kresenz, five years younger.[7] Both died before he did, Kresenz when he entered the seminary, and Elizabeth a few months before his own death. His fellow Redemptorists saw how much these deaths affected him.[8] He also witnessed the death of another sister named Babette. She died of typhoid fever when she was only ten years old.[9]

Stanggassinger's siblings later recalled how their brother often went on walks with them and prayed the rosary with them. When he was in high school in Freising, he brought them various sweets.[10] Yet he could also be strict with them, especially once when three of them, aged only between three and thirteen, finished off half a bottle of brandy that they had bought for their father.[11] This did not, however, cause them to hold a grudge against him since they admitted he had acted in their best interests.

On May 17, 1877, Kaspar entered primary school in Berchtesgaden. Not the most gifted pupil, he nevertheless was the hardest worker. This caused some of his classmates to think of him as ambitious. This drive came from his wanting to become a priest. In fact, he liked to "play priest." He built an altar and preached to the younger family members from a tree trunk. He was a happy individual and had the ability to laugh hard; but he avoided overdone pranks as well as scuffles with other children.[12]

It would be too much to see signs of a saint in his behavior since many other children acted as he did. Something, however, was special about him: even early in his life, Kaspar had an attraction to prayer. When someone was looking for him they often found him in the Kalvaria Chapel on the Fürstenstein.[13] When his mother told him of the sufferings of Christ, he burst into tears and was heartbroken.[14]

As to his wanting to be a priest, was it only a child's game that he would outgrow? In answer to this question, those who believe in the guidance of God can clearly see that something more was at work here. The youngster had decided to hear God's call at an early age.

Kaspar's leaning to become a priest was very clear from the beginning. The words of a two-and-a-half year-old, "A priest, this is what I want to become one day,"[15] may not mean much in themselves. But they gain importance when one traces the straight line that Kaspar followed to this goal—especially after November 21, 1880. For, as a priest, Stanggassinger was to make a list of the most significant days of his life. In his listing we find that date with a note that says, "Calling to priesthood."[16] He says he heard a call during Mass at the consecration.[17] Whatever happened to the nine-year-old on that day, thereafter he had only one goal. Along the way there would be many tests.

On September 23, 1881, Stanggassinger entered high school in Freising. For three years he lived in the house of the parish priest named Roth.[18] These years were not entirely filled with unspoiled joy. Kaspar was an "excellent student," but he did have difficulties, especially in mathematics. Thus, one of his teachers told him to go home and work on the farm.[19] Another suggested that he become a shoemaker.[20]

When his father heard of his low marks, he burst out in anger, "This is too expensive! If he does not have the talent, he should give up study! The pitchfork is what he should take up!"[21] During these years Kaspar often turned to the two sisters of the priest and begged, "Pray for me!"[22] Was he perhaps not called to the priesthood? Regardless, he would do his best.

In 1884, one of his deepest wishes came true when he was admitted into the minor seminary in Freising. His classmates liked the friendly and unassuming boy. "He imparted a heartfelt friendliness," they would say later. "Those who knew him, liked him ... He held his head high ... he was not a complainer." He was "quite amusing" and "could laugh heartily,"[23] even when a harmless joke was at his expense.[24] Of course, the cheerful boy had other qualities besides. He was sensitive, not indifferent to praise or to disparagement, and sometimes had a problem restraining his anger. If he was inwardly excited about something, this was obvious. Mostly he avoided discussions. But when it came to religious questions, if he did not agree he would state his opinion firmly but calmly.[25]

Stanggassinger's former classmates agreed in their assessment that there was nothing to criticize about his character. This does not mean that he was exemplary in every way. Rather he was natural and shared a normal student's smaller and greater joys and setbacks with the others, even if these were very human. His prefect said that he once found him deep in thought and asked him if anything was wrong. "Oh," he replied, "I was just wondering if there was going to be dessert today."[26] However, when it was appropriate to stand for something, he was decisive, even in smaller things. As the story goes, he always kept strict order on his desk, in his closet, and regarding his clothing. So it seems we can gather that his external orderliness indicated what was inside him.[27]

Many have given special emphasis to his sincerity. He preferred to receive a poor grade than to deny his convictions. One day his German literature professor proposed as a topic for an essay Schiller's *Bride of Messina*. Stanggassinger did not like the work and consciously interpreted the topic differently. This promptly earned him a failing grade for the assignment.[28] However, he did not have many opportunities to show such courage. In Catholic Freising, only Professor Hellmuth dared to defend liberal Catholic views, because the Bavarian Centrist Member of Parliament, Georg von Orterer, exerted his conservative influence here. The well-respected politician who taught Stanggassinger Latin in his third year called him "the most refined character among [my] students."[29]

Since Stanggassinger had entered the minor seminary, his performance in school slowly improved. In the fourth year, however, his teachers advised him that it would be more reasonable if he would repeat the year. Repeating was out of the question for Kaspar's father: "If he has to repeat a year, he proves that he is unfit to study. Then he has to come back home!" When the teachers heard of the father's reaction, they saw to it that Stanggassinger passed the year successfully.[30]

Kaspar Stanggassinger as a 12-year-old student

The family homestead: In the middle is the house where Stanggassinger was born; in the adjacent building on the left, Kaspar had his room as a student.

Stanggassinger as a seminarian
in Freising, 1887

Stanggassinger at age 19,
about to enter university studies

A family photo from 1890: Stanggassinger, center,
is shown with his parents, his grandmother, and fourteen siblings.
To the immediate left of Stanggassinger is his father, and to the right is
his sister, Elizabeth. His mother and grandmother are seated at the table.

Theology student in Freising, at age 20 or 21

This is Cathedral Hill in Freising, with the preparatory and theology seminaries in which Stanggassinger spent the first years of his studies for the priesthood.

In the fifth year, his grades improved. Tenacity and industry, which his report cards mention, eventually paid dividends. (Interestingly, it seems that homesickness during his first year in the minor seminary had lowered his grade for industry).

In the later years he excelled in religious studies, always with top marks. But he also did well in history and German, and this was duly recognized by his teachers.[31] They were delighted when the otherwise calm Kaspar spoke vividly and with style. As he grew older he caught up with the students for whom the studies came easily in the early grades. Success continued to elude him only in mathematics, which, he later confessed, he never did like.[32]

His success was found in other arenas. On a number of occasions, he played a part in the seminary's theater performances. His classmate, Josef Hofmiller, later acclaimed as a literary scholar, reported that Stanggassinger's performances were "not theatrical, but deeply moving."[33] Of his first stage experience, Kaspar, barely age 18, reported to his parents:

> Three days ago I was an actor. I played a servant of King Oedipus. The old Greek play, Sophocles' *Oedipus Rex*, was presented at the seminary. It was the first time that I performed in front of such a respected public. When we, the actors, arrived in the dining room after the performance, we were overwhelmed by the thunderous applause. However, now your Kaspar has retreated again into calm solitude.[34]

The last sentence of this letter indicates that outward success during these years was not essential for him. Rather, his "inner life" took first place. During these years a certain piety matured into a deep connection with God. There is no doubt that he was serious from the beginning, despite the fact that the external character of his piety seems to us only somewhat "enlightened."

Through the support of the pious sisters of the parish priest, Kaspar joined a number of religious groups, among them the Sodality of Mary. From these various groups he owned several medals, which he wore around his neck. At night, when it was quiet in the dormitory, one could hear the noise the medals made when he moved. His classmates teased him, saying that "the cow with the bells is going to bed."[35] This may have been a lesson for Kaspar. All his life, he was opposed to any kind of outward show of his personal piety. His classmates soon noticed that there was more depth to him than this. While they called him "the priest," or "the cleric,"[36] it was taken not as a nickname but as a mark of honor.[37]

Kaspar was careful not to draw attention to himself. He participated in the celebration of Mass every day, even during vacation time. He received Communion every Sunday, as was the custom in those days, and he spent many hours praying in the chapel. However, when it was time for recreation he happily took part and was in no way a killjoy.[38] Later he wrote of what may have been a mature realization: "In our first fervor we may want to see only serious faces. But God loves a cheerful giver."[39]

Aside from God's grace and his own intention to grow up, Kaspar owed his inner maturing to the leadership of exemplary and sensible priests. Among these were the theology professors at Freising, Michael Seisenberger and Francis Xavier Pleithner. Seisenberger, even while busy with his teaching, continued to be active in pastoral work. He founded the student Sodality of Mary at Freising in 1861 and still led this group in his advanced years. He wanted to give life to the faith of the students and to lend depth to their prayer life. To this end he requested of his students to receive the sacraments frequently, and he led them through the celebrations of the church year. His goodness and understanding heart helped so many to overcome the difficulties of youth. He proved to be consistently friendly and approachable. Stanggassinger, who joined the sodality as early as 1882, learned much from Seisenberger, carefully keeping notes of his lectures on the liturgical year.[40]

Yet he was even closer to Francis Xavier Pleithner, his theology professor. This man, too, was a director of the Sodality of Mary and was known as "mild, intelligent, patient, and selfless." The students of Freising looked to him as a confessor and advisor. He carefully guided many of them to the priesthood, but his method was not to exert any kind of pressure on their spiritual growth. He always showed understanding for those who chose a different path in life. As he led with benevolence, he gained the appreciation of all. When necessary, he could have a way of kindly making demands on the students. For instance, he insisted that daily participation in Mass was indispensable for future priests. Stanggassinger was among Pleithner's penitents and owed much of his religious formation to him.[41]

Three notable events influenced Stanggassinger's spiritual life. One was a general confession in 1887, which may have been his first. We will return to this presently. Then in 1889 there were two very different events. Stanggassinger recorded these among the most important days of his life.

He fell gravely ill in February 1889. It was probably an occurrence of typhoid fever, as many other records of his life suggest. However, meningitis cannot be excluded. For many days he remained unconscious, and the worst outcome was expected. When he finally did regain consciousness, he asked for his confessor, Father Pleithner. He made a general confession and received what in those days were referred to as "the last rites." Not long after, the director of the seminary, Doctor Stigloher, who had attended the ill Stanggassinger, wrote to his parents that for Kaspar the worst was now behind him. He was fully conscious and had regained his old sense of humor. When the nurse came to serve him soup, he laughed and quipped, "You found the smallest cup, didn't you?"[42]

On March 10, 1889, Stanggassinger wrote to his parents that he now "felt better than before the disease." To calm any fears, he described the menu to them:

Morning 5:15	– a cup of boiled milk and a roll
Morning 7:30	– a cup of coffee and a roll
Morning 10:00	– ham, wine and a biscuit
Midday 11:30	– soup, roast deer with sauce, beer (not quite a third of a liter) an entire roll
Afternoon 3:00	– coffee, entire roll
Afternoon 5:00	– approximately like 10:00
Evening 7:00	– soup, roll, veal with a steamed apple

He added: "This is how I am doing in the seminary. Don't worry about me."[43]

However, what was not mentioned in his letter to his parents is what happened inside him. He described his feelings in an article titled *Studentdank* ("A Student's Gratitude") in May 1889 that he wanted to publish in the *Sendboten des Göttlichen Herzens* (*Beacon of the Sacred Heart*).

> For a long while my heart has been filled with gratitude toward the Holiest Heart of Jesus. During the month of February I fell victim to a nervous fever. Already, at the beginning of my illness, the dear Lord planted in my heart the urge to seek shelter in the Heart of Jesus and that I should completely surrender my fate to him, whatever course my illness would take. I received the grace to receive last rites fully conscious. The day after the fever stopped I regained my strength. I can continue my studies. Thanks be to the Sacred Heart of Jesus forever.[44]

Out of gratitude, Stanggassinger offered himself and his life to the Heart of the Redeemer. At about this time, the word "conversion" can be found in his notes.[45] During his illness, did he experience what the recognized teachers of spiritual life call a "second conversion?"

In the same year of 1889, Stanggassinger experienced another event, one no less important than his severe illness. Very likely it was on the advice of his confessor, Father Pleithner,[46] that in August he took part in a retreat at Innsbruck. The retreat director, Father Francis Hartler, a Jesuit, had made a name for himself by his writings that promoted meditations on the Sacred Heart of Jesus. Hartler was also well-known as the editor of the *Sendboten des Göttlichen Herzens Jesu.* Stanggassinger opened his soul to the inspiration he received on this retreat.[47] For the rest of his life, meditations on the Heart of Jesus were important to his spiritual life.[48] The notes that he kept give us an insight into these meditations. He was not concerned with mere emotional piety, for as he wrote, this is "only blood and nerves."[49] When he dwelt on the heart of Jesus, he referred to the love of God who became human, and how the generous gift of self led to his death on the cross. From this time on, a Christocentric emphasis was a mark of his spiritual life.

Since Stanggassinger wrote a spiritual diary, we can follow the path along which God led him. It does not contain empty self-reflections, but testifies to a balanced, double-tiered program.

On the one hand, his diary shows how from his youth

Stanggassinger worked at developing an orientation of his person toward God. Throughout the diary we find a recurring question: "What good are beautiful ideas if they do not bear fruit in my life?" Consequently, he wished to "meditate practically." He wrote down simple mottoes and read them over and over.

On the other hand, he did not exhaust himself in do-it-yourself piety and asceticism. He knew that only "the Lord can build the house." In this context another peculiarity of Stanggassinger's spirituality comes to the fore. He wrote, "All must be caused by the Holy Spirit."[50]

As a sixteen-year-old he already prayed, "Holy Spirit, Spirit of Grace, never leave my heart! Stay with me, because as a poor man I cannot have a good thought unless you help me!"[51]

Stanggassinger repeatedly prayed for the gift of an attentive heart, not wishing to miss the voice of the Holy Spirit. He knew that the influence of God's Spirit is weakened if one is not alert to divine inspiration. His confessor advised him, "Don't be confused about this. Don't let up in your trust of the Holy Spirit."[52] Kaspar followed this advice to the end of his life, and during his academic trials prayed for the Spirit's gift of knowledge. Rather early his devotion to the Holy Spirit matured, as is shown by a meditation that he composed for Pentecost (probably in 1892). It belongs among his most beautiful and original writings:

Spirit of holiness, come into my heart.
Give me true holiness,
always to want and to recognize the good
and the true,
and to hate and despise what is evil and false.
I am poor without you.
But if you come into my heart with your grace,
then I am not poor, I am infinitely wealthy.
Only through grace do we arrive in heaven.
Only through grace can we grow better,
Only through grace do we remain good.
If God's Spirit is with you,
all is easy, all turns out well.
Holy Spirit, you are the light of bliss and brilliance
which reaches to us from eternity.
Without your grace I am nothing.
Give me your grace, and I will collaborate with you
When I am in your grace
I renounce everything else.
But when I proceed on my own, directing myself and
my affairs, then I shall fall,
because without your grace
I can do nothing.[53]

There remains one other thing about the piety of Kaspar as a high school student. His first biographers placed a large emphasis on this trait, but we have to ask how it really relates to his spiritual life. He is described as a "second Saint

Aloysius."[54] (In part this refers to the fact that in joining the Third Order of Saint Francis in 1888 he was "named" Aloysius in the group).[55] It is also sure that the description of Kaspar as a second Aloysius came firmly from what a saint was supposed to look like then. We also find him described as someone whose thinking is highly fixated on chastity and virginity—and this fixation is *not* borne out by the notes in his spiritual diary. Admittedly, in official documents we find the following: "He went about with eyes cast down, not even wanting to look at his uncovered feet unless he had to."[56] And it appears that the seminary director confirmed such when he claimed that Stanggassinger once, when reading a poem, was unable to say the word "love" when it did not refer to a theological virtue.[57]

Those closest to Kaspar in the seminary have firmly denied such comments. For instance, his classmate, George Huber, with whom he often discussed spiritual topics, says that the anecdote about "uncovered feet" is false. On the contrary, Stanggassinger considered it as strange to read in a biography of Saint Aloysius that he did not look at the face of any woman, not even his mother's.[58] Even as a priest, of course he looked at his mother's face, even if the novice master of the time thought, "Yes Father Stanggassinger is certainly pious and he was an exemplary novice. However, when it comes to this question, he should not be imitated.[59] Similar accounts are found in a biography of Saint Aloysius.

Stanggassinger's best friend, John Stadler, who crafted the love poem in question for a May celebration at school, has cleared up that issue. It was not Stanggassinger but the seminary director who objected to the line "time of pleasure, time of love." He wanted Stadler to substitute another word for "love." Stanggassinger then tried to help Stadler find another word. The try was without success, but Stanggassinger told Stadler, "You know the director, why not do him the favor? It would be a shame if he were upset over this."[60]

Based on such testimony, one may conclude that however much Stanggassinger belonged to his era of history, he did not fit the image of what a "saint" supposedly was in the nineteenth and early twentieth centuries. This is clear from his personal notes. No evidence of timidity is found there, although it was typical for many of that time, and not just in church circles. Without a doubt, celibacy held an important place in Stanggassinger's dedication to God. However, when he writes and talks about "purity of heart," he above all refers to an openness to God and God's love. After a study of all of his notes, we can conclude that Stanggassinger did not repress his physical ability for love into the realm of the subconscious. Out of a sense of a greater duty and a greater love he abstained in a mature and well-thought-out manner. At the age of sixteen and with the consent of his confessor, Doctor Pleithner, a reasonable and caring man, he took an oath of chastity.[61] But he did not lose any of his sincerity and genuineness. Rather, one had the impression that he had gained more freedom to dedicate himself to God and to others.

What about Stanggassinger's vacations? One thing we can say: they were not boring. Although witnesses to his life have little to report about his day-to-day school activities, they suddenly become wordy about the vacation times they spent with Kaspar in Berchtesgaden.

He did not just sleep or dream away these times of more freedom. Every day had three fixed events: Mass, one hour of study, and a walk up to the chapel above his father's property where he usually led the rosary. This visit to the mountain chapel was sometimes replaced with a longer hike up the mountains called Untersberg and Watzman.[62] And sometimes there were unforgettable adventures. Stanggassinger himself told of one time when he was frightened when suddenly, as he climbed a peak, giant eagles came swooping dangerously close to him.[63] His friend John Stadler told of another occasion when he himself overestimated his ability in the mountains. He became stuck on a steep cliff and was close to falling. Stanggassinger risked his life to rescue Stadler.[64]

Making a deep and lasting impression on Stanggassinger were longer vacation trips that he took with his good friends. These trips took him to Innsbruck, Merano, Linz, Wels, and to the Salzkammergut.[65] He gave a presentation on his Merano trip on January 6, 1890, at Freising.[66] And earlier, as a sixteen-year-old, he wrote about Innsbruck, where he had gone on foot from Garmisch in 1887:

> There are certainly a number of cities in the German-speaking countries which can measure up to the capital of the duchy of Tyrol, and maybe even surpass it. Even if their position on a river, on a lake, in a valley, or at the foot of a hill were more lovely, nowhere can one walk as

> in Innsbruck with the mighty Alps visible from each small street. Full of secrets and ceremony, the giants-become-stone absorb the events of the present with a barely audible hum. One would think that people would grow better and nobler as they face these millennium-old guardians, whose feet are firmly rooted in the earth—but whose peaks reach into the pure ether of heaven.[67]

These are the words of an adolescent whose encounter with the mountains of his homeland kept turning into an encounter with God.[68] These words also give away part of the secret of this graceful young man. He, too, was firmly rooted in the land of his Berchtesgaden home and in his family, with whom he stayed in close contact. He was genuine and knew the meaning of daily work. His heart, however, was turned toward heaven.

Other accounts of Kaspar's vacations are unusual. Here one can see hints of his later task as a leader of youth toward Christ. He was to become not only an example to later young seminarians, but he cared for them deeply. While he was not yet twenty, he became, so people said, the "father of the students." It started with helping young students in their Latin homework, acting as a tutor here and there, and taking students on tours through the mountains. Neither piety nor fun was shortchanged. In the early morning a small group would gather in church for Mass. The ensuing expedition would usually lead to one of the many churches dedicated to Mary, the Mother of God, around Berchtesgaden. The group would often pass his parents' house, or the house of a wealthy relative, where a meal would be waiting on the table for the young students. Kaspar made sure that their stomachs did not stay empty. Thus, he could dare to pray the rosary on the way or to visit a chapel in the mountains. None of the students thought they were forced into a religious mold, and all of them remembered the excursions with excitement.[69]

On August 7, 1890, Stanggassinger's high school period came to an end with graduation. His report card turned out rather well.[70] An important intermediate goal on his way to the priesthood had been achieved. At the graduation celebration on the evening of August 7, the graduate smoked his first—and last—cigar.[71] He went home the next day, with the graduation cap on his head. As always, Kaspar used the layover in Munich to visit his grandmother at the Herzog hospital church. Also in Berchtesgaden, his first visit was to the church. Then he bought a hand-carved statue of Mary, a copy of the one in Kälberstein before which he had prayed so often over the years to ask for success in his high school studies. Only then did he go home.[72]

ENDNOTES

1 Causa Mon. 192, 259; Zeugnisse 7, 36.
2 Causa Mon. 212.
3 Causa Mon. 261, Schriften V, 89F.
4 Causa Mo. 89, 196, 200, 211, 215, 259; Zeugnisse 7, 14, 36, 72.
5 Zeugnisse 14; Schriften V, 21f., 39-42, 59f., 67f.
6 Causa Mon. 162f; Zeugnisse 82, 190.
7 Causa Mon. 117, 162, 259; Zeugnisse 16f.
8 Zeugnisse 82f., 133.
9 Schriften V, 126; Causa Mon. 162.
10 Causa Mon., 161f., 199ff., 204.

11 Maria Kurz (Stanggassinger's sister), "Schnapsgeschichte," September 21, 1950, StAG.
12 Causa Mon. 158, 161f., 169, 322.
13 Causa Mon. 169, 175f.; Summarium 310.
14 Causa Mon. 333; *Meier* 8f.
15 Zeugnisse 87; Causa Mon., 164, 181; Suppl. 97.
16 Schriften II/2, 139.
17 Summarium 271.
18 Causa Mon. 320ff.; Zeugnisse 14.
19 Causa Mon. 162, 164, 166, 283, 359.
20 Causa Mon. 406.
21 Causa Mon.,164, 170, 196.
22 Causa Mon. 322.
23 Causa Mon. 152, 155, 163; Zeugnisse 144-47, 210.
24 Zeugnisse 6.
25 Causa Mon. 317; Zeugnisse 182.
26 Zeugnisse 13.
27 Causa Mon. 93, 118; Zeugnisse 7.
28 *Meier* 23.
29 Causa Mon. 238; Suppl. 32; Zeugnisse 18.
30 Causa Mon. 105, 320.
31 Schulzeugnisse Stanggassingers StAG.
32 Zeugnisse 75.
33 Causa Mon. 244; Zeugnisse 67, 69.
34 Schriften V, 13f.
35 Causa Mon. 301, 308; Zeugnisse 44.
36 Causa Mon. 98, 102, 106, 151, 292, 303; Suppl.33; Zeugnisse 120.
37 Causa Mon. 17.
38 Causa Mon. 119, 124, 127; Zeugnisse 113.
39 Schriften II/2, 15.
40 Six 26-9.
41 Six 30-3.
42 Causa Mon. 109, 118, 162; Schriften V, 15f.; Zeugnisse 30.
43 Schriften V, 17f.
44 Schriften I/1, 35f.
45 Cf. Causa Mon. 407.
46 Cf. Six 40.
47 Schriften II/2, 139. For Hattler cf. *Lexikon Für Theologie und Kirche* (2nd ed, Freiburg: Herder 1960) V:27; J. Hättenschwiller, *P. Franz Hattler, ein Herz-Jesu-Apostel unserer Zeit* (Innsbruck 1929)
48 Cf. Causa Mon. 164, 184, 199, 218, 330, 410; Schriften I/1, 18, 20, 24, 53f. 72; II/1, 27ff.; II/2, 97; III, 366, 372f.
49 Schriften II/1, 56, 116, 186.
50 Schriften I/1, 82f.
51 Schriften I/1, 22.

52 Schriften I/1, 72f.; cf. I/2, 8ff. (A meditation on the church year, probably according to Seisenberger.)
53 Schriften I/3, 155-67.
54 *Meier* 25, 87, 210.
55 He did not choose the name. Meier is mistaken in following Zeugnisse.
56 Causa Mon. 62.
57 Zeugnisse 20.
58 Causa Mon. 245.
59 Zeugnisse 144-147.
60 Zeugnisse, 120; *Meier* 215.
61 Causa Mon. 293f, 298ff; Zeugnisse 121.
62 *Meier* 55.
63 Causa Mon. 152.
64 Causa Mon. 115, 293; Schriften I/1, 37f., V, 35, 142; Schuster-Wildenauer 30ff.
65 Schriften V, 24.
66 Schriften I/1, 37f.
67 Cf. Schriften III, 98.
68 Causa Mon. 163, 182, 247, 293f., 298-300, 309f.
69 Abiturzeugnis, StAG.
70 Causa Mon. 106, 119, 128, 131, 182; *Meier* 30.
71 *Meier* 30f.
72 Causa Mon., 197.

CHAPTER TWO

AT THE SEMINARY

"Be afraid of the high peaks and do not aim for the extraordinary!"

The 1890 vacations were barely different from the previous ones. Notwithstanding the many hours he spent at the bedside of his seriously ill sister, "Zenzi,"[1] the young man collected impressions on long hikes and excursions with his friends. A long trip led him to Vienna and to a number of Austrian monasteries. However, Kaspar was disappointed. What he saw there did not match his ideas of monastic life.[2]

There was no doubt that he would enter the seminary after these vacations. However, he was subjected to the advice of well-meaning people to choose a different vocation. The vacationers stayed at the farm of the progressive Kälbersteinbauer family (which, by the way, was one of the first in Berchtesgaden to own a telephone.[3]) They didn't understand why the good-looking graduate wanted to join the priesthood.

The wife of the district magistrate, a somewhat eccentric countess, especially tried to change his mind. As a new graduate he had occasion to introduce himself to "Mrs. Magistrate." She congratulated Stanggassinger on passing his examinations and asked what field he had chosen for his future. "I want to study theology." "What? Study theology?" she asked, "But you come from a well-respected family. You are talented and you have excellent prospects. You won't have to worry about getting help for some prominent post." Kaspar waited until she was finished, and then said, "Ever since my childhood, I have wanted to become a priest; no other idea has ever entered my mind."

His friend, Stefan Blum, waited outside. Kaspar vented his anger about what the lady had said. Showing little respect, he said, "The bitch tried to convince me not to enter the priesthood." His friend remembered this phrase well, since he had never heard Stanggassinger ever utter the word "bitch." Someone like the "Frau Magistrate," however, was no real temptation. Kaspar was much too set on his plans.[4]

Less certain was where the new graduate would study theology. Friends of his father, especially the Bavarian nationalist Doctor Alois Ritter, a college director and member of the Bavarian parliament, advised him against Freising. Eichstätt had become the center of neo-scholastic philosophy, the place for authentic Catholic teaching. But not Freising, where Heinrich Hayd taught philosophy.[5] In his youth Hayd had encountered the writing of the legal scholar Wilhelm Rosenkranz of Munich who, with the best of intentions, had tried to synthesize Schelling and Saint Thomas Aquinas. Hayd was enamored of the teachings of Rosenkranz. As with Rosenkranz, Hayd was looking for the connection between Catholic doctrine and contemporary philosophy, a project that appeared suspect to "guardians of the Faith." But if some of his students misunderstood Hayd here and there, it was not the professor's fault.[6]

Stanggassinger, however, decided against Eichstätt in favor of Freising. He wrote, "I feel a childlike love for the Cathedral Hill area, which has been my second home for nine years.[7] And as far as Hayd was concerned, he would not become a threat to the student. While he thought that there was little use for Hayd's philosophy in the daily work of spiritual guidance,[8] he did not join the chorus condemning the sickly but good-hearted professor.

One day, when Hayd said in his lecture, "One wants to cry, knowing that so many thinkers stay away from Christianity," Stanggassinger agreed, coming out with a loud "Bravo!"[9] Naturally, the rediscovered philosophy of Saint Thomas Aquinas was more to his liking. As the eager Kaspar wrote, he was permitted to attend the classes containing the "blessed teachings according to Aristotle and Saint Thomas Aquinas, taught by the barely thirty-year-old assistant Sebastian Huber."

Stanggassinger was among the studious members who attended a special seminar within the "Thomas Aquinas Academy." For this he prepared several papers on "Knowing and Willing," "Is the Principle of Causality Based on Objective Reality?" and "Are Bodies Composed of Matter and Form?" On November 22, 1891, he gave a presentation at the academy titled, "The Position of Philosophy in Human Spiritual Life and Knowledge."[10]

But so as not to move ahead of our story, we note that on October 22, 1890, Stanggassinger formally entered the major seminary. Three days later, however, he returned to Berchtesgaden.[11] His beloved sister, "Zenzi," who was not yet fifteen, had died. She was known as an especially good and devout child. In January 1890, she had fallen ill and never recovered. During the Easter break her brother, Kaspar, had spent all of his time with her, trying to comfort her. There was a brief improvement, but in early May she was back in bed, seriously ill, and received the rites for the dying. Her brother was devastated by the news. He had written her a letter expressing the hope that, once with God, her joy would be unending.

Of course, he secretly hoped for her improvement, even when their mother told him that her pain was getting worse. Kaspar also comforted his mother: "Even if you do not get to church anymore, be assured that the dear Lord does not hold this against you. Give my heartfelt regards to my dear Zenzi and tell her that I surround her with my prayers for an early recovery." It seemed as if his prayers had been answered. In mid-June, Zenzi was able to get out of bed, and she replied to Kaspar's letter. He was delighted. "How I thank the dear Lord that he made you well again."

But her recovery was short-lived. She died suddenly. How much this death devastated him can be gleaned from a letter that he wrote shortly afterward to his family. "Neither you, my loved ones, nor I can ever talk to her and look at her again. She cannot be among us. All that is no longer possible." Then Stanggassinger has Zenzi say, "Don't cry! I am well taken care of."[12]

His sister's death was not going to be the only heavy blow during this period of his seminary studies. A year and a half later his grandmother died. As noted previously, she was a deeply religious woman with whom Kaspar knew a close relationship.[13]

According to his own words, Stanggassinger liked this time in Freising "as a fish likes water."[14] It is, however, understandable that he was looking forward to the end of his philosophy course. For one thing he found little that was useful and practical in philosophy. But also he had been pursuing the difficult subjects of biology, physics, chemistry, and world history. In those days those were university subjects (not found in high school, as is true today). Also required in the seminaries of both Munich and Freising was basic agricultural science, since each parish church had a farm.[15]

Max Westermaier, who was a scientist and a keenly religious man, taught most of his required subjects. He died in 1903 in Freibourg, Switzerland, while serving as a professor of botany. (In 1948 the process for his beatification was begun.)[16] Stanggassinger liked him very much, especially because he made his agricultural lectures into a "colloquium on interesting subjects" such as the theory of evolution.[17]

Finally his philosophy level was behind him. During his vacations Kaspar paid special attention to the Berchtesgaden students who wanted to be priests. He led excursions into the Salzkammergut and to the Danube.[18] In October 1892, he began his theology studies. "Last year," he wrote, "we had so many subjects, this and that experiment, chemistry, mineralogy, calorics, etc. I do not want to denigrate the importance of this knowledge, because it is necessary for a complete education. However, when the dear Lord has called you to study a subject which puts the experimental aspects far behind the speculative ones, it is good for the soul to stay closer to the spiritual subject."[19]

His favorite subject was dogmatic theology.[20] This is no surprise, since the deeply religious professor Francis Xavier Pleithner understood this subject to mean the conveying of a living faith instead of dead knowledge. He gave Stanggassinger a grade of *Excellent.*

> What made me feel especially comfortable about his genuine piety was his happy personality. He was always joyful and always in the mood for a joke. He was very talented in dogmatic theology. In his first semester, I gave him a top mark with the note of *Excellent.* If I gave him only an "A" in his second semester, it was because I did not want to give him any kind of preferential treatment that could be ascribed to my genuine affection for him.[21]

For Kaspar, there was no shortage of top marks with a note of *Excellent.* He got one in New Testament biblical exegesis with Professor Seisenberger and in church history.[22] The lectures by the seminary regent Gundlach were "truly outstanding." Stanggassinger was "deeply moved" when Gundlach respectfully and sadly told of his teacher Johann J. Döllinger in 1870, who came into conflict with the Church because of the dogma of infallibility.[23]

Aside from his studies, Stanggassinger found time for research on the history of his homeland. In the Berchtesgaden regional paper, *Der Watzmann*, he published a treatise about the origins of Berchtesgaden.[24] Among his papers can also be found an essay on the Church in the thirteenth century, apparently intended for publication.[25]

All this hardly distinguished Kaspar from the other students in the Freising seminary. Everyone tried very hard to make progress. Maybe Stanggassinger was more industrious than many of his colleagues, but more importantly, as his teachers and friends testify, he was happier.[26] Behind this happiness, however, there was hiding a deeply introverted man. One senses this "inner brilliance," but it was not overpowering. What he wrote to his parents, and what he composed for his sister, Zenzi's, gravestone also applied to him. Some family members objected to the fact that the then-customary gravestone phrase, "pious virgin," was missing. But Stanggassinger explained, "Those who knew her do not need reminding on her gravestone that she was a pious virgin. We are what we are before God. "All the splendor of the king's daughter is within."[27]

At that time a new chapter in Stanggassinger's "inner life" was about to begin. As a student of philosophy he obtained the classic ascetical work of the Theatine priest Lorenzo Scupoli, *The Spiritual Combat*, a text that would accompany him until his death. The many notes in his book are evidence as to how much importance Kaspar ascribed to the book. The student Stanggassinger started *The Spiritual Combat* deliberately.[28] Notes that start on October 31, 1891, and end on June 1, 1892, three days after Pentecost, offer glimpses of his inner life. At the beginning there are notes and plans from the retreat at the beginning of the semester. Then there are spiritual notes, which Stanggassinger jotted down after morning prayer. Each of them ends in a short resolution for the day. Especially impressive are the notes during the preparatory retreat for minor orders in the spring of 1892. Also impressive is the systematic and consistent work on himself. He fulfilled his resolution to hold a day of recollection each month, and in such a manner "that no one notices that you are doing your recollection today."

When we read randomly his spiritual notes from this period of his life, we notice how this grace-filled young man focused his entire being on the love of God and a loving devotion to God. He was later to write, "I want to *be love*, or not be at all." But such a sentiment is foreshadowed even in these earlier notes.

Likewise, the reader is struck with how thoroughly, when he was yet a student, he was led by faith. He lived in a world of faith and moved securely in that world, seeing all in the light of faith. However, his asceticism was not separated from reality. There was no false effort, nothing strained.

Even more clearly than the spiritual diary written in his high school period, these notes composed as a theology student exhibit, so to speak, two poles of his inner life. The first is a radical determination to follow Christ with all his strength, with absolute devotion. The second is a simultaneous awareness that all growth in love for God and other people is a result of pure grace.

Stanggassinger was also conscious of the way of purification: mortification of the senses, of the eyes, the ears, and the tongue. He resolved to avoid any unnecessary chatter, to avoid asking questions just out of curiosity, to forego things consciously in order to purify his heart, to free that heart for God's grace. He realized that, when it came to scholarly discussions, he leaned strongly in the direction of insisting on his own views. But then he resolved to hear the opinions of others, to value them, because "they too have their good reasons." His motivation in this was a great respect for others, but he also recognized that "the more a man knows himself, and the more one steps back, all the more can one love God."

All of this was not to show itself in extraordinary deeds. His asceticism focused on small things in everyday life, for example, on faithfulness to house rules and the conscious use of time. At table and when taking walks he resolved to be friendly. Likewise, he vowed to take his studies seriously. It is noticeable how he shunned any kind of exaggeration: "Be content with small progress and do not reach too high! *Be afraid of the high peaks, and do not aim for the extraordinary!*"[29]

On April 2, 1892, Stanggassinger received what in those days were referred to as "minor orders" as a cleric of the Church. He wrote in his diary, "I became a cleric through the grace of God. Once a priest, I will look back on this day, especially when it will be time to die. Oh my God, preserve in me true fervor, and provide me with your grace!" He resolved to close "the many doors and windows of the senses" to the noise of the world in order to look for God with even greater determination. A series of daily prayer exercises would preserve this fervor.[30]

As in every other year, Stanggassinger traveled to Berchtesgaden in the summer of 1892 for his vacation time. Neither his teacher, nor his fellow students suspected that he had left Freising, and the Cathedral Hill area, so dear to his heart, forever.

ENDNOTES

1 Zeugnisse 16.
2 Schriften V, 35.
3 Communication Wildenauer, StAG.
4 Causa Mon. 83, 163; Zeugnisse 42, 72, 187.
5 Causa Mon. 83, 151, 239f., 244, 298; for Rittler cf. K Möckl, *Die Prinzregentenzeit* (Munich, Vienna 1972) 572f., 68.
6 Mayer 94f.; M. Joachim, *Memoiren eines Obskuranten* (Kempten 1896) 829f.; ADB 29 (1889) 208-13; ADB 50 (1905) 84–7; Hayd's followers probably included Stanggassinger's discussion partner on his walks, George Huber, the "dark philosopher." Cf. Causa Mon. 239f.
7 Schriften V, 33f.
8 Schriften V, 50.
9 Causa Mon. 245.
10 Causa Mon. 240, Zeugnisse 7; *Meier* 36; to Sebastian Huber, Mayer, 75.
11 *Meier*, 35.
12 Causa Mon. 117; Zeugnisse 16f.; Schriften V, 24, 28f., 30, 32, 39f.,151.
13 Zeugnisse 14; Schriften V, 21f., 39-42, 59f., 67f.
14 Schriften V, 53.
15 Semesterzeugnisse, StAG.
16 J. Koller, *Forscher und Christ, Prof. Doctor Max Westermaier 1852-1903* (Freiburg in der Schweiz, n.d.) 169.
17 Schriften V, 64.
18 *Meier*, 68f.
19 Schriften V, 63f.
20 Schriften V, 63.

21 Zeugnisse 31.
22 Semesterzeugnisse, StAG.
23 Schriften V, 63f.
24 Schriften I/1, 1-6; V, 70.
25 Schriften I, 7–10.
26 Zeugnisse 31.
27 Schriften V, 53. This quotation in German seems to be of an old version of Psalm 45:13. Modern versions are different than this.
28 Exemplar Stanggassingers, StAG; Schriften I/1 82-9.
29 "Annotationes," Schriften I/3, 1-133.
30 Schriften I/3, 103 ff.

CHAPTER THREE

ON HIS WAY TO THE MONASTERY

"Father, this is what I must do!
I must become a Redemptorist."

Stanggassinger counted September 12, 1887, as one of the most significant days of his life.[1] A few days earlier, in the pilgrimage town of Dürrnberg near Hallein, he had made a general confession with the Redemptorist Father Anton Höfer. We do not know the contents of this meeting. However, after he had read the monthly prayer for "vocations to the Congregation" in the *Sendboten des Göttlichen Herzens* (Beacon of the Sacred Heart), "the thought to enter the Redemptorist Congregation never left him." "Soon," he reported later, "the thought vanished only to return even stronger,"[2] especially when he made the pilgrimage to the Mother of God in Dürrnberg to visit the monastery there. Upon his return, his family found him lost in thought. His relatives would say, "Today you visited the Redemptorists again; no one can talk to you." Or, "Today you look rather like a Redemptorist. One of these days you will stay there. Watch out! They want to snare you."[3] They were not entirely wrong. The Congregation was in urgent need of young people, and it may well have happened that Father Alois Straub, a man of imposing stature and great power of conviction pushed him to "become a Redemptorist!"

With Stanggassinger, such efforts would usually have the opposite effect. He insisted, "I will be free in such a choice. I will not let anyone take me by surprise."[4] Neither by the Redemptorists in Dürrnberg, nor by the Franciscans in Berchtesgaden, nor by the Capuchins in Altötting. It had been with these Capuchins that he was once deeply moved in witnessing the Order's Investiture Ceremony.[5]

The idea of the Redemptorist Congregation did not leave him alone and "often overwhelmed him deep in his heart."[6] And, "From the fullness of the heart the mouth speaks." (Luke 6:45) Stanggassinger often spoke of the Dürrnberg Redemptorists at his seminary. On such occasions, he often heard the protest: "They do not fit in with Bavaria. They are too much Italian." He did not think so![7] He often told his colleague, Ludwig Eisenhofer, who later made a name for himself as a professor, that no other Congregation was better suited than the Redemptorists to solve modern problems of pastoral care. The same Eisenhofer also reported that, on a visit to Dürrnberg with Stanggassinger, he had been kept waiting and waiting for the latter at the entrance to the monastery. His friend, Kaspar, was having a very lengthy discussion with Father Matthias Baumgartner. When he finally appeared at the door, Eisenhofer said, "I think they want to keep you. I, of course, would consider only the Benedictines."[8]

When it came time to enter the major seminary in 1890, it seemed that Stanggassinger's desire to become a Redemptorist was overwhelming. During his vacations, he visited the Redemptorist monastery of Maria am Gestade in Vienna. This is where Saint Clement Hofbauer, sometimes referred to as the "second holy founder" of the Congregation, had found his final resting place. Kaspar had read Clement's biography with enthusiasm. Now he was able to take a relic of the saint with him. On his way back, he visited the Redemptorist monastery in Leoben, in the state of Styria. He felt much more welcome in these monasteries than in other monasteries of his travels.[9] If, however, there was any hesitation on his part to join the Congregation, his family's negative attitude (especially his father's) may have played a part.[10] But his own sense of unworthiness could likewise have been at work. For him the Redemptorists were exemplary priests, in particular the venerable Father Joseph Schnall.[11] Schnall passed away in 1890, and Stanggassinger was often to pray at his grave in Dürrnberg.

No doubt Stanggassinger had loved Freising. But he later admitted, "From the first time I put on clerical clothing, I wanted to exchange it for the habit of the Congregation of Saint Alphonsus."[12] He opened up only to his confessor, who tried to sway him neither one way or the other, stating, "If it is God's will, God will see to it that the divine will becomes reality." Kaspar kept to himself his thoughts about joining the Congregation. Yet he continued preparation for diocesan priesthood as though he had already taken vows in the Congregation. What he wrote in his spiritual diary on May 29, 1892, strongly indicated this tendency.[13]

In mid-September 1892, he and his friends went on a mountain hike on Watzmann Mountain. His friends remembered that he was even happier and more relaxed than usual. In the bitter cold he knelt in front of a picture of the Virgin Mary to pray the rosary. Also, despite the exhausting hike, he did not neglect to pray his breviary.[14]

Afterward the group of friends traveled together to the monastery in Scheyern, and there they separated. Stanggassinger, as he had done so often previously, wanted to visit the Chapel of Grace in Altötting before the academic semester started. As he was praying in front of an image of the Mother of God, he believed that he had heard Mary's voice inside him, "Go to Gars to the Redemptorists!"[15]

Despite the fact that he had not fully made up his mind, he immediately traveled to Gars am Inn to visit Fathers Höfer and Baumgartner, whom he knew from Dürrnberg. When the fathers went for their evening meditation, he stayed in the visitors' room alone. What happened then he describes as follows: "Without having had the chance to speak with someone about the daily life in the Congregation or my vocation, the infinitely merciful God enlightened me about life in the Congregation, so much so that I could no longer resist." There, he realized, "a life with God, in God and for God" would become possible. Only then did he open a small book that he had received titled *The Vocation to Life in the Congregation* by Alphonsus Maria de Liguori, the founder of the Redemptorists. His reading confirmed his thoughts. Soon afterward he went to Father Provincial Anton Schöpf's room. Stanggassinger informed him that he wanted to become a Redemptorist.[16]

From Gars, Stanggassinger traveled to Freising. On the way he visited his fellow student, Balthasar Berndl, who would become the parish priest of the future Cardinal Ratzinger (Pope Benedict XVI) in Edling near Wasserburg. Stanggassinger did not tell him of his plans.[17] In Freising, Stanggassinger went to Regent Doctor Georg Gundlach and told him of his decision. Gundlach answered simply, "I am not surprised by your decision. Since I have known you, it was clear to me that one day you would come to this decision."[18]

The first hurdle was crossed. But there were some additional obstacles to overcome. Stanggassinger traveled to Munich to ask Archbishop Anton von Thoma for permission to leave the diocesan clergy. The Archbishop showed little understanding. "I need hardworking people for my own diocese," was his first reaction. Then he asked for three days to think about the request.[19]

Stanggassinger went to Arget near Sauerlach, where his kindhearted friend, Georg Roth, worked as a priest. It was here that he wanted to wait for the bishop's final decision.[20] He notified Father Provincial in Gars, who immediately wrote to the bishop on September 29, testifying to the genuine nature of Stanggassinger's calling and strongly supporting his request.[21]

The aspiring Redemptorist soon learned that the Archbishop was not the only one in opposition. Father Roth in Arget also showed little understanding for his plan. "We tried to dissuade him because his theological studies had not yet been completed," Roth reported.[22] In the meantime, Stanggassinger's former prefect at the minor seminary, and later his professor, Max Heimbucher, came to Arget. He, too, could not understand why Stanggassinger wanted to join the Redemptorists before finishing his studies. He asked him to delay entering the Congregation in consideration of his family's, and especially his father's, opposition. Stanggassinger responded decisively that he could no longer resist the call of God.[23]

In the meantime, Father Provincial's letter had reached the archbishop, who no longer hesitated to grant Kaspar's request. On October 1, the release from the diocese, the so-called "dimissorial letter," was issued.[24]

This, however, turned out to be only a prelude. As soon as he had received the dimissorial letter, Stanggassinger left Arget and traveled to Berchtesgaden on October 4, 1892. The young theologian had expected some form of encounter there, but what happened exceeded his fears.

It was evening when Stanggassinger entered his parents' home. He greeted his mother and told her that he wanted to become a Redemptorist. The mother was devastated. She surely knew about the secret wishes of her son, but she had been hoping that as a diocesan priest he could help with the family's burdens. They had been experiencing financial difficulties. Only a short time before, some horses had died. The farm was deep in debt and they had to take out a mortgage. They thought that if Kaspar was to become a diocesan priest, one of his many sisters could move in with him as housekeeper, and so she was hoping that at least one of them would be taken care of.

His mother was crying, but she soon calmed down and said, "Whatever you think, son. It is better to be a good religious priest than an unworthy one of a diocese."

The major obstacle, however, was yet to be faced: How could the father be convinced? Every evening the family knelt to pray the rosary. As the prayer ended, Kaspar, still on his knees, turned to his father and asked him for his blessing to enter the monastery. The reaction was fierce. The Redemptorist Provincial Schöpf reported later that his father acted "like a madman." That is all they needed. Aside from his economic difficulties, he had political problems. The local newspaper *Der Watzmann,* which he had supported financially, had been taken over by its rival *The Berchtesgadener Anzeiger*, which meant a loss of political influence for him. If the son went over to the Redemptorists, who were considered enemies of the "*Reich,*" he would lose more prestige.

"How did you even get such an idea?" his father shrieked. "Until now you have provided me with a sense of joy—at school and at the university. You have cost me a lot of money. A few more years and it will all have been worth it."

Kaspar, still on his knees, answered, "Father, I have to do this, I have to become a Redemptorist."

His mother tried to mediate. "Father, why not say yes! You will see we will be doing better again." But the father remained adamant: "Leave me alone! I say no!"

The conversation went back and forth for some time, until finally the siblings, desperate, who were kneeling on the floor, started to get involved. "Why don't you let Kaspar go?" they pleaded.

More than an hour went by. The parents sent Kaspar's brothers and sisters out of the room while he kept kneeling on the floor. Then the father said, "I will not give my consent. Come, get up!"

Kaspar quietly rose and went to his room. He did not sleep that night. The next morning around four, he awakened his siblings. With a burning torch in hand he led them to the Chapel of the Virgin Mary on the Kälberstein. There they prayed the rosary together. Then they all went to their father and asked for his approval. He still could not hide his anger. It may have been a ray of light for Kaspar when his father said, "I am not giving my approval—not yet. As far as I am concerned, you can go wherever you want."[25]

The next day, Saturday, October 6, Kaspar rose early. His mother prepared breakfast for him. He did not speak to his father anymore; what could he have said? He had made him an outcast, Kaspar later confided to a confrere.[26] However, he did not think that it would take some years until his father would agree completely and entirely. Later he did indirectly receive a telegram in which his father's acquiescence was communicated. This telegram was sent not by his father but by an uncle in hope of appeasing Kaspar.[27] A year later his father supposedly visited his son. Then on the occasion of his son's profession of vows, his father expressed approval.

Later, on his son's patronal feast day, he came every year to the monastery in Dürrnberg.[28] Finally, in May 1899, Stanggassinger could write, "My father is now entirely reconciled. [Until now] it would not have seemed entirely right if I returned [to ask his blessing]."[29]

On his deathbed in 1911, his father said, "Kaspar was my favorite."[30]

ENDNOTES

1 Schriften II/2; Zeugnisse 8f.
2 Schriften II/1, 2; II/2, 97.
3 Causa Mon. 120, 163, 183, 198, 209.
4 Zeugnisse 202.
5 Cf. Causa Mon. 88, 304, 321.
6 Schriften II/1, 2.
7 Causa Mon. 241.
8 Causa Mon. 120.
9 *Meier*, 67f., 115; cf. Causa Mon. 102 ; Zeugnisse 8f.;Schriften V, 35.
10 Causa Mon. 93, 115, 159, 179.
11 Suppl. 50; *Meier* 116; for Schnall : J.B. Frankenberger, *P. Josef Schnall aus der Kongregation des allerheiligsten Erlösers* (Passau 1891).
12 Schriften V, 85.
13 Schriften I/2, 72; cf Büche 30.
14 Causa Mon. 84, 198, 304; Summarium 271; Zeugnisse 35.
15 Causa Mon. 84, 198, 304; Suppl. 100; Schriften II/2, 177.
16 Schriften II/2, 7; V, 93; Suppl. 100; Schöpf to Generalate, October 25, 1892, GAR, P.G.S. IV B 8.
17 Causa Mon. 106.
18 Zeugnisse 19.
19 *Meier* 117.
20 Cf. Schriften V, 75.
21 Schöpf to Archbishop von Thoma, September 29, 1892, Abschrift GAR, P.G.S., IV B 8.
22 Zeugnisse 15.
23 Causa Mon. 93f.
24 Dimissorien, StAG.
25 Causa Mon. 163f., 176, 183, 198f., 205, 213, 216f., 231, 332;Zeugnisse 8, 50; Summarium 56f. (=Schuster-Wildenauer 58ff., Communication of Maria Kurz,

May 24, 1950, StAG); Schöpf to Generalate, October 25, 1892, GAR, P.G.S. IV B 8.

26 Causa Mon. 390.

27 Causa Mon. 163, 198; Schriften V, 84.

28 Causa Mon. 164; Summarium 197.

29 Schriften V, 126, 129.

30 Causa Mon. 27.

CHAPTER FOUR

IN THE NOVITIATE

"You shall have only one thought: to do the will of God."

Beginning the evening of October 6, 1892, Kaspar Stanggassinger was a novice at the Redemptorist monastery at Gars am Inn. At first he did not yet wear the Congregation's habit. He was free at any time to leave the monastery. But Stanggassinger had been testing himself for years. He knew the Congregation he had just joined better than any of his former fellow students in Freising.

He did not share some of his friends' or his father's prejudices against, or outright dislike of, this religious Congregation. These prejudices were to some degree quite understandable. As late as 1891, one could read in the newspapers about the exaggerated strictness of the Redemptorists.[1] There was also the issue of their previous expulsion from Germany, together with the Jesuits, in 1873. Moreover, those who had followed the negotiations in the Bavarian provincial parliament regarding the pending return of the Redemptorists must have thought it was not a matter of *Germans* who were returning, but of "dark foreign types."[2] Stanggassinger knew better, and he found himself in agreement with the Bavarian government, which had quietly tolerated the Redemptorists in the country since 1890.[3] Consequently, two priests, Fathers Anthony Höfer and Matthias Baumgartner, had returned to Bavaria from the Austrian town of Dürrnberg. In Gars am Inn, across the border in Bavaria, a novitiate was opened.[4]

But who were the Redemptorists among whom Stanggassinger sought and found his spiritual home?

The Congregation was founded by Alphonsus Liguori on November 9, 1732, in Scala near Amalfi in the Kingdom of Naples. The goal of the new religious community was the pastoral care of the poor and abandoned, those who had little or no pastoral care, mainly people who lived in rural areas.[5] If, however, workers in big cities found themselves with no religious contact or were overlooked by the Church, then the Redemptorists realized that they had a new challenge. None other than Pope Leo XIII told the Bavarian Baron of Crailsheim, at the time when Stanggassinger joined the Congregation, that he expected a great deal from the Congregation in the pastoral care of workers.[6]

The Congregation always remained true to its goal—to care for the abandoned whether in its native Naples or north of the Alps where the first German-speaking Redemptorist, Clement Maria Hofbauer, the "Saint of Viennese Romanticism," had transplanted the Congregation.[7] After many fruitless attempts, the Congregation was finally accepted by the Austrian government in 1820, and soon the "Liguorian Congregation," as it was known at that time, spread throughout Europe and America. However, it found its way into the geographical area of today's Germany only in 1842. The establishment of the first monastery in Altötting was followed by other establishments in Bavaria and in the Rhineland. The fathers worked mainly as popular missionaries, and it did not take long before the newspapers were full of stories of their appearance. Papers close to the Church celebrated them, while the liberal papers called them "un-German," "unenlightened," and too folksy. One could also read that they were "unbearably strict."

Such a judgment was not entirely groundless. If many of the fathers could be seen as examples of a holy Christian life, others often lacked sensitivity. These were the ones who tried to promulgate the rigorous principles of the monastery living within their pastoral work. Contrary to the teachings of their founder Liguori, they too often were scaring people away rather than converting them to the love of God. Nevertheless, the ban against them in Germany was unjustified. Two things helped these men moderate their very strict views and their callous methods of pastoral care: first, their interaction with other confreres during times of exile, and secondly, their enforced periods of self-reflection.

It was Father Provincial Anthony Schöpf, the leader of the Southern German Redemptorists, who dealt the first blow to such spiritual strictness. His men recognized that benevolence and humanity did not contradict a pious and holy life, but actually completed it. This was in accord with the spirit that Stanggassinger would bring into the monastery from Freising.[8]

Stanggassinger was overjoyed to be at Gars am Inn. The day after he arrived he wrote to one of his teachers in Freising, Doctor Sebastian Huber: "What great grace, what joy! I cannot say anything else, and I ask for your holy prayer." Then again on October 23, "It is heaven on earth, a second paradise." He wrote to his parents on October 26, "If you look at the step I took from the point of view of faith, you must be happy from the bottom of your heart. Be happy along with me, because I feel so good here! I have not regretted for a moment that I followed the voice of the Lord."[9]

On November 29, 1892, Stanggassinger was invested with the habit of the Congregation. He was happy. The day after, he wrote: "Thank God and Mary. Yesterday, our dear God, in his unending grace, and by the prayer of the Heavenly Mother, presented me with the habit of the Congregation of Saint Alphonsus, my religious father. What a beautiful and great day!"[10]

Stanggassinger also found joy in belonging to a community that seriously tried to follow Christ. The person of the novice master, Father John Frankenberger, contributed in no small measure to this joy, for he was generally regarded as a saintly man. It was said of him, "Anyone who saw the old man with his snow-white hair, his benevolent face and his downcast eyes was deeply moved. He loved spiritual talks. When it came to worldly topics he was quiet in holy meditation... He used all of his free time for prayer. He prayed the Way of the Cross daily. He prayed the breviary kneeling before the Blessed Sacrament. He always was attending the celebration of Eucharist."[11] The new novice felt safe in the "fatherly, loving care of the honorable, old, white-haired novice master."[12] As we can see from his notes, Stanggassinger listened to the words of the experienced monk with an open heart and he allowed himself to be guided on the way to holiness. This is not to say that he accepted everything uncritically.

Father Provincial himself once criticized Frankenberger as "unfortunately too one-sided in some matters. He is fond of private revelations." Indeed, Father Frankenberger invariably gave lectures on Mary in connection with the revelations of the mystic Mary of Agreda, whose *Mystical City of God* he almost "knew by heart."[13] Thus it is even more surprising that Stanggassinger, despite the novice master's guidance, went in a different direction, the way of humility and of daily faithfulness to the will of God. Even in the novitiate he lived according to the principle that he later stated: "Many have reached salvation without prophecies, ecstatic experiences, signs, and miracles, but no one without humility."[14] He already had the maturity to know and to cling to the insight that:

> High secrets are not for you. Stay with the basic dogmas and examine them and not "revelations!" They often lead you to doubt, because they often contradict each other. The essential is the gospels. We do not need details; they only make us curious. The saints have had special enlightenment. Therefore, we should not look down on these revelations. For me, who is not a saint, they are incomprehensible. Therefore I stay with the simple truths:

> eternity, becoming human, redemption, and the Most Holy Sacrament.[15]

In the novitiate, Stanggassinger wanted nothing to do with "false mysticism." He also thought that to show piety one did not need to run around with a frown on one's face. "A human being must be happy," he wrote at the beginning of his novitiate, "otherwise he cannot live. Sadness shortens life."[16] Stanggassinger did not lose any of his natural friendliness and happiness, even when he seemed more introspective to some of his visitors.[17] His cordiality did not diminish; it matured. One felt that it came from an inner center. And with his cordiality a second quality matured, which consistently was later described by witnesses of his life as "understanding others." This was not easy, since Stanggassinger soon learned that one goes to the monastery to look for God, but finds things that are all too human.

With Stanggassinger in the novitiate was an assortment of personalities. Joseph Schleinkofer was a man of boisterous character; yet he later would render great service to the Congregation as a religious writer and an eloquent, popular missionary. People would say he competed with Stanggassinger to fulfill the requirements of novitiate life and that he was jealous of Stanggassinger's apparent ease over any hurdle.[18] Then there was Max Müller, a thirty-eight year-old former financial office assistant from Ottobeuren. He had in fact wanted to be a brother rather than a priest. But since he had attended Latin classes the provincial was of the opinion that he should study theology after the novitiate, which he did.[19] Müller once wrote about his fellow novice:

> Stanggassinger gives one the impression of a truly happy novice, completely comfortable with himself. Aside from good health and a good intellect, he possessed a strong penchant for self-denial. Add to this a fact which should not be underestimated: his former life in the major seminary in Freising. He was always focused on his current task.[20]

There was also a former law student from Stuttgart named Eugene Mahlbacher; he was to die quite young in December of 1898 in Brazil.[21] And there was a novice who did not fit in well with others, although the superiors held him in high regard. Apparently he knew how to make a good appearance, and he gained attention in the monastery community with his "water therapies." Once before he had received the Redemptorist habit, chose to leave from Redemptorist life—only to be readmitted in October of 1892. A report on him is ominous: "Through flattery and begging he succeeded in being readmitted, and this wolf-in-sheep's-clothing nearly chased away all the sheep, the novices among the ones to whom he caused bewilderment.[22]

It was Joseph Schleinkofer in particular who decided he could no longer stomach the peculiarities of the "good and talented" fellow novice. When he told Stanggassinger about his struggle, the latter simply replied, "Someone cannot possibly remain the same. I hope he will change one day."[23] But

Stanggassinger's real sentiments became more definite shortly before he died: "How I thank God that I was supported in the grace of my vocation. However, I, too, was tempted to run away when I was in the novitiate—all because of a confrere who knew how to fool the novice master."[24] In fact, we can see from his notes—even if the confrere is nowhere named— that Stanggassinger seriously questioned if he was meant for life in the monastery. However, they also show that he continued his resolve to endure the faulty and chafing ways of others. "Look at yourself," he repeated to himself, "and there you can find enough shortcomings. And he realized that "even if there were only saints living together, they would cause each other grief."[25] Still, he and the other novices were probably relieved when on July 7, 1893, this strange fellow novice interrupted his novitiate year because of nervous problems, never to return.[26]

Most of what happens in the novitiate takes place in solitude between God and the novice. So as far as we are concerned, the deepest dimension of the inner life of Kaspar Stanggassinger remains hidden. But we can try carefully to grope our way into those depths by poring over his notes. They underscore the reality involved in his and all genuine religious quests: Anyone who chooses to follow the path to God with all one's heart knows that in this endeavor one is carried along by God's love.

Thus, there is no contradiction, but it bespeaks the classic way to God when a novice continually tells himself, "I can, I will, I must be holy."[27] Or, when he undertakes concrete acts of mortification. Or, when he engages in set prayers. Or when he is persuaded, "The Holy Spirit must be the source of everything, especially for a religious, and even more especially for a novice." Stanggassinger knew that "you can do nothing of yourself; everything is God's grace." But he also knew, "God's grace is not magical." Faith was crucial for him and so was absolute trust in God.[28]

In these notes another quality is evident in Stanggassinger's asceticism: his determination and drive are ceaseless but never seemed forced. He was steadily guided by good sense, and he let himself be led more and more by the grace and spirit of God. "Do not move forward too fast!" he advised himself, "everything step by step." Another time he planned "not to leap ahead."[29]

In the retreat before his reception of the habit, Stanggassinger sketched out the path he wanted to follow. He was convinced that he could best fulfill God's mission for him in a monastery. The many devotional books he had brought to get closer to God did not seem to satisfy his heart. He seemed to be disaffected by all the things he read that he had brought from outside. This occasioned the remark, "Here you do not need a book anymore, except for the sacred Scripture and the breviary." He made an exception for only one other book, namely, Scupoli's *Spiritual Struggle*, a book in which he wrote many notes during that novitiate year.[30]

In his own religious life leading up to his novitiate, Stanggassinger placed a high value on clearly defined goals that did not leave anything to accident. The novitiate provided him with the opportunity to move farther along in this direction. He wrote that he intended to proceed "methodically." Free from distraction and work, he had plenty of time to practice basic exercises that would help him to open his heart to God. Above all, he also made use of the daily examinations of conscience, the general examen and the particular examen, as were customary in the monastery. The concentration was on a single shortcoming one wanted to root out, or on a special virtue one wanted to acquire. Stanggassinger believed that pride and self-love were his main shortcomings. He thought that he discovered self-complacency and too much sensitivity in himself. Therefore he intended to become "more humble, selfless, and more trusting in God."[31]

To his regular examination of conscience he added something that is virtually unheard of today. It was called in German "*Der Wandel in Gottes Gegenwart.*" In translation it means a "Conscious Change in the Presence of God." In those days it was a rather common practice and was well-recognized and praised by those of ascetic bent. Stanggassinger, a child of his time, probably believed that if the method was used with measured virtue and prudence, it could help one toward a mature and well-structured spiritual life.

He engaged as often as possible during the day in brief, repeated prayers. He also wanted to combine all of his daily actions with a faith-filled sense of God being with him. Thus, when rising in the morning, which in the cold at Gars was not always easy, as he washed and dressed, he would pray certain prayers. He was aware that his novitiate year was a never-to-be-repeated opportunity. One time a Redemptorist priest said to him, "One can reach only that degree of holiness for which, at the beginning of his spiritual life, he has established a foundation." We can also find this idea in his notes. And this may have been the motivation for his wish to add a second year to his novitiate.[32]

Despite some things that may appear strange today, and which may be linked to his frequent headaches,[33] Stanggassinger was, overall, on the right path. This conclusion may be garnered from a close reading of his notes. From the many forms of meditation of which he spoke when in high school, he slowly found his way to a certain unity and simplicity. Even when he saw some of the prayer exercises as helpful, finally only one thing became important to him. "You shall have only one thought: to do the will of God."[34] Then, God took him at his word. Soon he no longer felt any God-given excitement when praying.[35] It seemed that he had been able to pray better and taste delight before entrance into the monastery. Now he felt only distaste "in prayer, spiritual reading, Communion, and even recreation." And so he discerned with great awareness: "True peace of soul consists in this: doing the will of God even when God leaves us in despair and darkness."[36]

Securely and with a clear goal in mind, Stanggassinger embarked on the way that teachers of the spiritual life, especially Saint John of the Cross, had already described. The works of this great Spanish mystic were not yet familiar to Stanggassinger. Yet the young Redemptorist's notes seem to read like a practical commentary on the saint's ideas. For example, he reflects that for him the way to perfection cannot be found in certain religious exercises or in beautiful feelings. Only one thing is necessary, "to learn how to deny oneself, inside and out, in all earnestness, in order to be ready to suffer for the sake of Christ and to mortify oneself in all aspects." Saint John of the Cross added, "True progress can be found only by following Christ." This could lead as far as feeling rejected by God. "It is uncontested that in the hour of his death Jesus felt completely rejected, even destroyed, since his Father left him in utter 'dryness' and without any comfort."[37]

The end of the novitiate year arrived. His superiors assured Stanggassinger that they were convinced of the genuineness of his vocation to the Congregation.[38] His novice master wrote to the Congregation's headquarters in Rome:

> Frater Kaspar Stanggassinger, a student in minor orders, with a very good mental disposition, showed in his novitiate life such noticeable industry that he was regarded as an example by his fellow novices. His great progress in knowledge and in his inner life allow us to hope that in his future life in the Congregation he will remain a pearl and that he will render great service to the Congregation.[39]

The retreat in preparation for his vows took place from October 1 to 15, 1893. Stanggassinger wanted to keep the intensity of the novitiate in his later life at the monastery. Therefore he wrote down some simple religious principles that were to accompany him. They were the fruit of his meditations; everyone could use them as a guide.

I am worth only as much
as I am worth before God.
He who loves God can find comfort
and joy in all things.
In order to lead an inward life,
one must worship the Holy Spirit.
When the mind is stormy,
pray until it calms down.
Conscious change in the presence of God is
the ABC of the inward life.
One who is master of one's inner self
does not encounter 999 temptations of the
1,000 of someone who is distracted.
Long-term sadness is not a good sign;
therefore always be happy!
God alone is good.
What people call good in creatures is God's mercy.

There is no art in kneeling before God and receiving spiritual comfort. However, to perform the most varied work, and, in doing so to perform the will of God happily, that is a great blessing for which one must pray.

It is not a monk's duty to be perfect. However, it is his duty to strive at all times for perfection.

Through faithfulness in small things, the saints became holy.[40]

Since it was impossible to profess vows in public in Germany because of the Redemptorists' banishment, the novices Schleinkofer, Mahlbacher, and Stanggassinger left Gars on September 29, 1893. Their destination was Dürrnberg. During the ascent from Hallein to Dürrnberg, Stanggassinger remembered a psalm he had prayed during mountain hikes while he was a high school student: "*Who may go up the mountain of the LORD? The clean of hand and pure of heart*" (Psalm 24:3–4).[41]

Stanggassinger professed his vows in the Congregation on October 16, 1893, in Dürrnberg. This was the day on which the feast in honor of Gerard Majella, a Redemptorist brother who had been beatified by Pope Leo XIII, was celebrated for the first time. Kaspar wrote in his spiritual diary that evening: "The eternal union with God has been sealed. Now I belong completely to God and the Holy Mother of God, to Saint Alphonsus, and to the Congregation of the Most Holy Redeemer."[42]

ENDNOTES

1 Cf. *Rheinischer Kurier* (Wiesbaden), December 24, 1891.
2 Cf. Weiss 376ff., 390ff.
3 Weiss 394.
4 Schöpf to Generalate, October 25, 1892, GAR, P.G.S. IV B 8.
5 Cf. T. Rey–Mermet, *Le Saint du siècle des lumières: Alphonse de Liguori (1696-1787)*, preface by Jean Delumeau, (Paris : Nouvelle Cité, 1982). Summarized in part in T. Rey-Mermet, *Moral Choices, The Moral Theology of Saint Alphonsus Liguori,* translated from the French and edited by Paul Laverdure, (Liguori, Missouri: Liguori Publications, 1998).
6 Weiss, 407.
7 Josef Heinzmann, *Preaching the Gospel Anew, Saint Clement Maria Hofbauer,* translated by Bernard J. McGrade, edited by Paul Laverdure, (Liguori, Missouri: Liguori Publications 1998).
8 Weiss, passim.
9 Schriften V, 76, 78, 81.
10 Schriften V, 83.
11 *Meier,* "Lebensbilder," PAG; cf. Weiss 683f.
12 Schriften V, 78.
13 Visitation report by Schöpf, November 26, 1890, GAR, P.G.S. IV A 5a; Weiss 683f.; cf. Schriften II/1, 145–80.
14 Schriften II/1, 233.
15 Schriften II/2, 67. Stanggassinger remained true to this opinion. Cf. Summarium 134. To his student Karl Härle he said: "I always pray: 'Lord, preserve me from mortal sin and mysticism!'": Causa Mon. 284.
16 Schriften II/2, 109.
17 Zeugnisse 35.
18 Zeugnisse 201. Schleinkofer diary 224, 231; Schleinkofer personnel file PAG. For Schleinkofer : J. Schuster, *P Joseph Schleinkofer, Lebensbild* (2nd ed.: Cham 1932).
19 *Meier,* "Commentarii 1911," 56–62.
20 Suppl. 67; Zeugnisse 96f.
21 *Catologus CSSR* (Rome 1898) 104.
22 *Meier,* "Commentarii 1911," 59f., "Notizbuch" StAG, Schöpf to Generalate, October 25, 1892, GAR, P.G.S. VII B 3; Frankenberger's Report, GAR, P.G.S. VII B 3.
23 Zeugnisse 159f.
24 Zeugnisse 102.
25 Schriften II/2, 21, 24, 190.
26 Schöpf to Generalate, September 10, 1893, GAR, P.G.S. IV C 2. Frankenberger Report, (as in note 22).
27 Schriften II/1, 117, II/2, 14, 33, 73, 142.
28 Schriften I/1, 83; II/2, 2, 18, 33, 48.
29 Schriften II/2, 14, 17.

30 Schriften II/2, 82–9.
31 Schriften II/2, 1–7, 11-21; II/1, 223.
32 Schriften II/2, 213ff.; Causa Mon. 391f.
33 *Meier* 212; Schriften II/2, 22f.
34 Schriften II/1, 91.
35 Schriften II/2, 6, 8, 16.
36 Schriften II/1, 92; cf. II/1, 116, 186.
37 Johannes vom Kreuz, collected works in five volumes. Volume 1: *Aufstieg zum Berge Karmel* (5th ed., Munich 1957) 102f.
38 Cf. Schriften, II/1, 92.
39 Frankenberger's Report, GAR, P.G.S. VII B 3.
40 Schriften II/2, 49–51.
41 Causa Mon. 327, cf. Schriften I/1, 37.
42 Schuster-Wildenauer 77f.; cf. Schriften V, 94f.

CHAPTER FIVE

IN THE STUDENDATE

"Thorough study helps us toward a purity of faith."

After his profession of vows, Stanggassinger entered the studendate. He was one of twenty theology students who were educated in Dürrnberg by experienced fathers in the preparation for their special pastoral work as Redemptorist missionaries. There were a number of new things for Stanggassinger. The contents and the teaching of theology were quite different than what he was accustomed to in Freising, especially regarding dogmatic theology. Without a doubt, his professor of this course was a highly talented individual who had studied theology in Freiburg and in Tübigen. The fact that he was guided by Saint Thomas Aquinas and the scholastics was welcomed by Stanggassinger, who had been a former and eager member of the Thomistic academy in Freising. But there was another problem; theology was taught in Latin and it was often dry.[1] What is more, Professor Louis Rieger showed a lack of understanding for his students' struggles, often complaining to the superiors about their "laziness and lack of ability." Given these circumstances, Stanggassinger had difficulties at first. But after a short time he overcame these, and Rieger learned to appreciate him. Rieger told the Dürrnberg rector, "I address my teaching only to Stanggassinger and Kiermeier. The others just slow me down."[2] When the provincial, Father Schöpf, visited the studendate in September 1894, he pronounced Stanggassinger and three other students "very talented, very good."[3]

Among the Dürrnberg teachers, Louis Rieger was the most eminent personality. Not only was the transmission of knowledge important to him, but, as he said, what was more important than all "book knowledge" was a clearness of thought and the inner application of what was learned. Stanggassinger was visibly impressed by Rieger. His goal in the novitiate had been to point his religious longings, his will, and his heart all in one direction. So now Rieger's training him to think may have helped to apply his intellect in matters of faith, and thus to balance out any one-sidedness. Furthermore, Rieger, influenced by the negative experiences of some of his confreres, was cautious in the face of all private revelations, allowing only the Gospel and theology to carry weight.[4] He was responsible for developing in Stanggassinger a healthy evasion of all mystical experiences.[5]

Rieger's presentations to his students and Stanggassinger's notes cast a light on this teacher, as well as on this student who was trying mightily to train his intellect. We read, "To study without a pen in one's hand does not help much." Or, "A lot of reading alone does not make a man intelligent, but only much thinking." And still further, "One must not abandon a subject until one has completely understood it."

It was typical for Stanggassinger to note all the comments of his teacher who challenged them to see the connection between theological study and religious life. Both belonged together. "Thorough study helps to keep faith pure," Kaspar wrote. However, he also penned these words: "He who studies theology without praying will easily become a dangerous fool."[6]

However much Stanggassinger accepted Father Rieger's training in thought processes, he must have been happy when practical theological subjects were put at the heart of his studies. These included moral and pastoral theology and a module for introduction to ministry. Theory for the sake of theory was not his realm. He hungered for active ministry.[7]

What happened to his novitiate resolutions when he reached the studendate? Now that the more devout and quiet atmosphere of the novitiate year was over, these resolutions had to stand a time of testing. They stood the test so well that his fellow students wondered, "Will he be able to continue as before?" Eventually they had to admit to themselves, "If any of us had made a vow always to be more perfect, the vow-maker could not have been more fervent."[8]

Obviously his religious exercises did not increase in number. They may actually have decreased. But Stanggassinger did not place any value on spiritual laziness. He knew that even his studies could lead to prayer. A few brief guidelines helped him arrange his daily work schedule so that he would still have time for God, and his spiritual life would not grow cold and stagnant. These guidelines then became an integral part of his daily examination of conscience.

God was still the center of his life. Led by his faith, his inner life grew more true, deeper, more clear, and more simple. "You must reflect on things in a spirit of faith, with living faith. You must pray simply. In the psalms you will find the most beautiful prayers. Your time of meditation must not be only *your* activity; God must be active in this time as well."[9]

In their simplicity, the results of his time of meditation appear quite valid in a timeless way:

God alone is worthwhile.
Anyone who loves God agrees with
whatever God wants.
We must ask God for stronger love,
rather than for tender love.
Our inner life is our real life.

Stanggassinger knew that true interior life had to be tested in everyday circumstances. It is not surprising that a fellow student said, "Punctuality and exactness in observance of the rules of the Congregation were a matter of course with him."[10] However, what his fellow students noticed most of all was his cordial, friendly way. "He always seemed in good spirits. He enjoyed putting himself second. He performed acts of kindness. He was friendly even to those who must have gotten on his nerves."[11]

Behind such behavior was more than a sunny disposition. We can see in his notes how his natural happiness and empathy were integral to his personality. He continually reminded himself, "I want to love my confreres. I want to be friendly, patient, peaceful. I do not want to get on anyone's nerves because of my peculiarities...I want to consider my words. I do not want to preach. Others get annoyed." If at all, he wanted to convince them by example, not with words.

"Do not judge! God accepts your confrere with mercy and kindness. Be full of love for him." He especially tried to overcome any hint of irritability or pompousness. Therefore, he told himself, "When a confrere draws your attention to a mistake, do not be offended, but be thankful."[12]

Such principles grow in importance when one considers the many clerical characters in Dürrnberg. Not all of them were pious like Father Moisl, who died of tuberculosis while in college, and whose obituary stated, "He constantly meditated and prayed."[13] Only a few could be said to be truly outstanding in character, like Stanggassinger's friend, Lawrence Hubbauer, who later became novice master in Brazil.[14] Others stood in contrast, and about these Stanggassinger, who usually never spoke ill of confreres, once said to a friend from former days in Freising, "Some of them I do not like." "Only later," said the friend, "did I understand his words. These confreres left the Congregation."[15]

On the other hand, superiors and those who conducted provincial visitations by and large were able to give good reports on the students.[16] Only after his ordination to the priesthood would Kaspar's love for his confreres be tested as severely as in the novitiate.

On September 28, 1893, Stanggassinger was ordained

subdeacon in Regensburg.[17] When in 1894 the Bavarian Redemptorists found a new area for their ministry, namely in Brazil, Kaspar Stanggassinger also volunteered for the foreign missions.[18] He wrote in his notebook, "You have a chance to go on the foreign missions. Remember how necessary it is that you be a strong spiritual human being....Therefore, train your inner life with renewed vigor."[19] Soon thereafter the Redemptorist Congregation was readmitted to Germany after twenty-one years of absence.[20] Good priests, and those with Stanggassinger's abilities, were needed at home.

Stanggassinger was ordained to the diaconate also in Regensburg. Bishop Ignatius von Senestrey of Regensburg officiated at the ceremony on September 21, 1894, in the presence of a small circle of confreres in the bishop's chapel. The following day, Stanggassinger assisted at the ordination to the priesthood of two of his confreres. One of them, Father Alois Meier, would become Stanggassinger's colleague in the seminary and his first biographer.[21]

Stanggassinger was ordained a priest on June 16, 1895, in the Regensburg cathedral.[22] He had prepared for years for this day. During the retreat prior to his ordination, he developed a program for his life as a priest. At the center was holy Mass. He organized his day around it; he wanted to draw strength from it. He strongly resolved to celebrate the liturgy daily and completely, and he wanted to avoid any "semblance of mechanical routine without complete devotion." For his pastoral work, he drew up clear guidelines:

> I am a priest because of God's love. I want to surrender completely to God's holy will and I will let my superiors do with me whatever they decide, be it to teach, to become a missionary here or in other parts of the world. I am only a tool in God's hands. With God's blessing I become everything to everyone. Should I have the choice, I prefer to preach to the poor, the ignorant, and the humble and lead them to God. In my sermons, I will avoid all clichés. Only in this way will I preach the Word of God and not myself.[23]

On June 24, 1895, Stanggassinger celebrated his ordination in his hometown of Berchtesgaden. The provincial had given permission only reluctantly. It was usual with the Redemptorists that the new priests celebrated their first Mass in the monastery. It was due to the request of the Berchtesgaden parish priest that the Redemptorists made an exception for Stanggassinger, since they hoped that such a celebration would be of pastoral benefit. Besides, it was an opportunity for the father of Stanggassinger to be reconciled with his son's entry into the Redemptorist congregation.[24] It would also be an indication to him and to the people of Berchtesgaden that the talk about the Redemptorists' excessive strictness was not true.

It was Stanggassinger who wanted this celebration at home the least. He would have preferred to pass the day quietly.[25]

For Berchtesgaden, it really became a day of celebration. Early in the morning came the boom of small cannons. The church was magnificently decorated, although too small for the number of people who wanted to attend. The sermon was delivered by Father Louis Rieger. Lasting ninety minutes, it dealt with the "blessings of the priesthood." During the Mass there was "so much violin and organ music that the people's ears were ringing." Lunch was served along with the playing of festive classical music in the grand hall of the Vier Jahreszeiten hotel. Even the superintendent of the local government took part and offered a toast for the new priest.[26]

All this was not to the liking of Father Stanggassinger. But as much as he would have preferred to withdraw from the noise, he took pains to disprove the Redemptorist reputation as austere people hostile to everything human. "Twice," he wrote, "I made the rounds to greet my relatives during the meal, simply to show them that the Redemptorists are not sinister people."

What he liked more than such external "compulsory exercises" that day were his own inner experiences and the meeting with certain people. In the courtyard he found time for silent prayer before lunch, and also to pray at the graves of his sister, Zenzi, and his grandmother. He was able to visit the hospital of the Sisters of Mallersdorfer, whose superior, Mother Solana, had accompanied him on his way to the priesthood with advice and prayer. He was especially happy that he could lead the evening meditation to the Sacred Heart of Jesus at five o'clock.[27]

However, a moment of sadness entered the joy of the day. As Stanggassinger might have preferred a more subdued celebration, he was indeed happy to be among his parents and brothers and sisters. Then he realized his sister, Katharine, was missing. When for a brief while he was alone in his room she came in and threw herself to floor, inconsolable. Then his mother entered, and she was crying as well. Finally she was able to say that Katharine was pregnant. Stanggassinger asked her if she had gone to confession, and then got up and blessed her. "She is full of remorse and that consoles me," he wrote on his first day as a priest. Still, he was shaken.

What hurt him the most was that some of his relatives, even his siblings, would not truly forgive her. People gossiped indignantly about "the dishonor and the shame which hit such a well-respected family." Thus, Stanggassinger wrote to his family on July 7, 1895:

> God has forgiven her and it has been a long time that she, on her knees, has asked you for forgiveness. And you, too, have forgiven her. Forgive her completely. For God's sake, do not be so hard. We may hope that in the sight of God she has been pure for a long time, even if the world does not know this. Do not be annoyed by people's gossip.[28]

On the evening of his first Mass celebration, he wrote to his provincial, Father Anthony Schöpf:

> Today is over. I just finished praying Compline. I have retreated to my room and I thank our Blessed Lord with all my heart, his holiest Mother and Saint Alphonsus for the great blessing he has given my poor soul. I could never have guessed what it is to be a priest at the altar if I had not experienced it myself. I was trembling so hard that I could not trace the cross with straight lines over the

Hostiam Puram [pure white host on the altar], despite the fact that I really tried to control my hand. It is true that I am now in my room full of wreaths and flowers, with more wreaths on my door—and a double triumphal arch stretches through the house. I am in my family home. Yet it all seems strange to me, as I would prefer to be in my monastery "cell."[29]

ENDNOTES

1 *Meier* 135f.; for Rieger: Weiss 700f.
2 Gebhard Wiggermann to Schöpf, Dürrnberg, May 29, 1894, StAG.
3 Visitation Report by Schöpf, January 18, 1894, GAR, P.G.S. A 5c.
4 Weiss 700f.
5 Causa Mon. 284.
6 Schriften II/1, 240.
7 *Meier* 135.
8 Zeugnisse 158ff.
9 Schriften II/1, 221.
10 Schriften II/1, 117; II/2, 90, 92, 95.
11 Zeugnisse 158ff.
12 Schriften II/1, 220ff., 225.
13 Untergehrer 52ff.
14 Cf. Summarium 159.
15 Causa Mon. 120.
16 Visitation Report, GAR, P.G.S. VI.
17 *Oberlichtes Verordnungsblatt Regensburg* (1893) 152.
18 "Nomina eorum ...," August 18, 1893, GAR, P.G.S. IV C 2.
19 Schriften II/1, 222.
20 Weiss 405ff.
21 *Oberlichtes Verordnungsblatt Regensburg* (1894) 146f., Untergehrer 33.
22 *Oberlichtes Verordnungsblatts Regensburg* (1895) 65f.
23 Schriften II/2, 95ff.
24 Dekan Widmann, Berchtesgaden, to Schöpf, February 26, 1895, StAG; Untergehrer 34.
25 Causa Mon. 426.
26 Sebastian Seidl to Schöpf, June 26, 1895, StAG.
27 Schriften V, 100ff; *Meier* 144f.
28 Schriften V, 102, 106ff.
29 Schriften V, 100.

CHAPTER SIX

COMPANION OF YOUTH

"I will gladly welcome everyone as if I had nothing else to do. God sends them all."

Kaspar Stanggassinger had decided to go where he was sent. And he was taken at his word. He wanted pastoral work and the preaching of parish missions. And hardly any of his confreres doubted that he would soon be active in these missions. He had a full and strong voice, and he was eloquent... but his superiors were convinced that he was needed more at the juvenate, the minor seminary in Dürrnberg.[1]

There he became instructor of the second class in Latin. He had to teach mainly German and Latin. At the same time he was in charge of teaching religion to all of the classes. After a short time he was promoted to the position of prefect[2] and became responsible for the junior students who lived in the so-called "upper house." He also had his room there, while the director, Father Joseph Wildgruber, lived in the "lower house."[3]

The Dürrnberg juvenate was the training ground for the next generation of southern German Redemptorists—but not for long. Before their exile from Germany, diocesan priests and theology students had joined the Congregation. So a minor seminary did not seem necessary.

But even during their exile, following the example of other Redemptorist provinces, the provincial superior started to train the next generation. A preparatory high school was begun in 1883 in Bachham (near Heldenstein in Upper Bavaria), and this was followed by a minor seminary, also in Bachham. However, since the Bavarian government did not approve of this minor seminary, it was moved to Dürrnberg in the province of Salzburg, Austria. In Bachham, only the students of the most junior classes continued to be taught, and it was done in secret.[4] The Dürrnberg seminary, with eleven students in Latin grades four and five, had been founded on September 29, 1886.[5]

As early as 1888, there were candidates for the novitiate coming out this juvenate. Most were not older than seventeen. They proceeded to be invested in the habit at Gars am Inn. But from Gars they were sent back to Dürrnberg, Austria, to avoid retaliation by the Bavarian government. The Congregation did without the state-sanctioned high school graduation certificate.

The schooling in this Dürrnberg juvenate was at first rather imperfect. Older priests, who had never taught in a high school, were employed as teachers. Consequently they felt overwhelmed. The attempted solution was to bring in young theology students fresh from their novitiate to teach the classes. With a half-Austrian, half-Bavarian curriculum, they managed the situation for better or worse. In 1883, by concession of the Bavarian cultural ministry, the students were allowed to take the examination required for entrance into Bavarian universities. It was becoming clear that much improvement was needed in this situation, as only a few students were equipped to meet the challenge.[6] Student numbers quickly increased. In the year that Stanggassinger started as a teacher, the Dürrnberg school had seventy-four juvenists. Of course, all were boarders, as was the custom for such minor seminaries.[7]

The transition to the juvenate was not easy for Kaspar. How he felt when he started teaching showed in the words he used when he introduced himself to his students: "I come to you as your teacher. This is God's will. I would have liked to go on the missions. But now I am responsible for the important task of training missionaries."

Stanggassinger knew what he had to do as a good religious. He wanted to accomplish his task as well as he could even if it was not what he had really wanted. This does not mean, however, that he would not tell anyone his preference. On occasion, he asked his superiors to release him from his job, since he did not think that he could live up to the task. But he was told he had to stay,[8] because he really was a good educator without realizing it.[9]

His provincial recognized this and after a short time wrote to the Redemptorist authorities in Rome that he regretted he could not use Stanggassinger on the missions. He was, however, an excellent teacher and prefect whom the boarding school could not afford to let go.[10]

At the juvenate, his charisma, which had already been noticed in his high school years, developed considerably.

He had outstanding sincerity, helpfulness, adaptability, and sympathy. These were the characteristics that stayed in students' memories.[11] They hardly thought that holiness could be found in these qualities, since at the time the Redemptorists associated holiness with strict asceticism, an ivory-tower mentality, and an unbending seriousness. Were saints really so generous, so human as Stanggassinger? Some of his students thought that Stanggassinger was the best superior one could imagine. He practiced the virtues more than most of the other fathers, but to them the old novice master Father Frankenberger seemed a better candidate for sainthood.[12]

At the Dürrnberg high school, one of his colleagues who had sat next to him at table and lived next to his bedroom for years, wrote:

> In those days nobody ever said that Father Stanggassinger would ever be beatified. People saw him as a nice and friendly priest. In my lifetime, I have met a number of priests, members of the Congregation, and lay people who may have exceeded Father Stanggassinger in holiness. However, Father Stanggassinger exceeded all of them in the fact that his virtue was extremely kind. He was modest, respected by everyone, loved by everyone.[13]

His students remembered Stanggassinger as a kind educator, or, as his father provincial said, "good of heart." It was a sympathetic goodness shown to everyone that had nothing to do with a weak nature or a shallow friendliness. His goodness combined decisiveness and clear direction, characteristics that stood out in this educator. However, such goodness did not come naturally to Stanggassinger. He had to do work for it, and his intent was to become an educator like Saint Francis de Sales and Saint Philip Neri.[14] From Francis de Sales' biography, which accompanied him to his deathbed, he took one sentence to heart: "With one spoonful of honey one catches more flies than with a barrel of vinegar." He often repeated the words of Philip Neri, "They may chop wood on my back as long they do not commit any sins."[15] Thus he matured more and more into the kindhearted teacher his students respected and loved. "He rid himself of some of his toughness when dealing with others during his years as a priest," wrote his high school colleague and biographer Father Alois Meier.[16] It was not always easy. Some of his students reported that one could see how he had to control himself.[17] And only a few weeks before his death, Stanggassinger wrote, "I want to overcome my vehemence. Otherwise I scare them away. Even criticism must be kind."[18]

To say yes to the students, to accept them, to like them—Stanggassinger saw this as the basis of all education. This attitude was more important for him than any pedagogical method. But he would not have been himself had he not continued to think about how he could be even better at his work. There are three things to underline here.

Stanggassinger took the basics of his pedagogical method and condensed them into short, easy-to-remember maxims that he kept pondering. One of these maxims demonstrates clearly the attitude of the teacher Stanggassinger: "If someone knocks at my door, even if I already have had to interrupt my work several times, I will not show any impatience. Rather I will gladly welcome everyone as though I had nothing else to do."[19]

Also, Stanggassinger did not see the responsibility of a teacher as different from the life of a religious and a Christian. Once he told a colleague that it is appropriate for a minor seminary teacher to review his duties as an educator during his examination of conscience. And he acted accordingly.[20] Furthermore, he did not take up important decisions without consulting his confreres, nor without praying for divine guidance.

Finally, to be a good teacher, he resolved to continue his own education. He told one of his students that he could well imagine making a depth study of pedagogy.[21] In this he was well ahead of his time. Special training in pedagogy, now common for teachers, did not exist then. He therefore had only one option, to read well-known pedagogical reference books. In this regard Stanggassinger was fortunate in his choice of authors. The book by the French Bishop Felix Doupanloup, *On Education*, became his regular companion. This work was the result of the author's long, practical experience as director of his high school in Paris, and as a professor of theology. It presented a balanced, enlightened program of ideal Christian education; the program aimed at instructing the intellect along with a training of the will and emotions. It shunned coercion and rote-memory while supporting the free development of a student's talents. Doupanloup saw this as the main task of a teacher whose personal devotion to the student was essential. The most important goal of education was "to help develop the heart." Young people should not obey blindly, but with help and insight.[22]

Such pedagogical principles were unusual at the time, in public institutions as well as in church boarding schools, and especially in Dürrnberg. Shortly after Stanggassinger's arrival in Dürrnberg, the director, Father Henry Stracke, was dismissed. He had striven to transform the minor seminary into a miniature monastery. Timid and stubborn, wanting only pliable "juvenist saints," he was ill-equipped for the post of pedagogue.[23] Under the new director, Father Joseph Wildgruber, the situation in juvenate did not change overnight. However, he quickly did away with the post of "zelator," whose task it was to encourage his fellow students to greater zeal for rules, and, failing that, to spy and make reports on his fellow students to the authorities.[24]

Some of the current customs taken from monastic life remained. Among them was the "Rule" of the North German Redemptorists that became the basis of the 1892 "Juvenate Rule."[25] Thus, Stanggassinger's biographer Joseph Schuster (who was among Dürrnberg's students at the time) has been correct in pointing out that the new prefect had "to reshape the spirit of education." And Schuster continues, referring to Stanggassinger, "this was maybe his most difficult task, more so because he himself had a leaning toward strictness."[26] Later we will return to this topic of seminary education among the Redemptorists.

As for Stanggassinger, his study of the works of Doupanloup certainly made his task of "reshaping" easier. When one ponders what he wrote down in his notes, the direction he set becomes more clear. And when we compare his notes with the text of Doupanloup, two things stand out: the first is how selective from Doupanloup he was. For Stanggassinger omitted those ideas of Doupanloup that were pertinent strictly to the bishop's own era. Secondly, Stanggassinger made an independent assessment of Doupanloup's original work: a number of the original pages are often condensed into one succinct sentence. Stanggassinger viewed these single sentences as simply a teaching guide. This was not only confirmed by his colleague, Alois Meier, but can be found within the lectures of Stanggassinger. Certain of these "selected thoughts taken from Stanggassinger's reading" are of interest even today:

> *God educates us as human beings. However, we humans are great instruments which God needs for our salvation.*
>
> *Certainly, one must encourage pupils without overtaxing them. One must urge them onward without coercing them. One must guide their will, and be able to help develop their conscience and their heart, without forcing them with violence.*
>
> *It is much easier to penalize than to convince someone that a mistake has been made, and that this mistake should be removed from the heart. It is simpler*

to threaten than to show the right approach. It is more comfortable to strike than to persuade gently.

What the educator does is a small part of education. What is most important is what the educator allows to be done, and what is done.

One cannot educate a young person without, or against, the young person's will.

There are two ways to ruin a young person: exaggerated strictness, and overindulgence.

One must not become violent in education or become hurried. Let us never forget: for young people forgiveness is always closer to justice than to strictness.

If one dedicates oneself to the work of education, one needs to have an unlimited supply of charity, patience, and dedication.

Tough strictness cannot possibly penetrate the heart, and really this latter is the most important aspect of education.

One should not obey as a result of violence, but as a result of love; that is, obey not because one must, but because wants to.

The basic groundwork of education remains as unchangeable as the center of a circle. The application of education to life changes constantly. A young person is also a free, moral, and reasoning being. One has to respect this. We cannot tie up a young person as a gardener might fasten a tree planted near a wall.[27]

ENDNOTES

1 *Meier* 146; Zeugnisse 123.
2 *Meier* 146; Causa Mon. 270; Summarium 252.
3 Causa Mon. 266, 270, 329, 430.
4 Weiss 336.
5 Franz Vogl to Generalate, October 15, 1886, GAR, P.G.S.III A 5.
6 Weiss 421f., 768–72.
7 PChr 86, PAG.
8 Causa Mon. 209; *Meier* 244; Schuster–Wildenauer 124; Büche 39.
9 Causa Mon. 142, 325.
10 Visitation Report, March 14, 1896, GAR, P.G.S. B 2.
11 Causa Mon. Passim.
12 Causa Mon. 352, 430.
13 Zeugnisse 208.
14 Causa Mon. 251, 279f., 283; Zeugnisse 22.
15 Causa Mon. 222, 227.
16 *Meier* 155.
17 Causa Mon. 317.
18 Schriften II/2, 136.
19 Schriften II/2, 99.
20 Zeugnisse 201.
21 Zeugnisse 24.
22 F.-A. Dupanloup, *De l'education en général,* 3 vol., German ed. *Die Erziehung* (Kirchheim 1867). For Doupanloup see C. Weber, *Liberaler Katholizismus* (Tübingen 1983) 42-55.
23 *Meier*, "Lebensbilder," Heinrich Stracke, PAG.
24 Carl Dilgskron to Generalate, September 23, 1897, GAR, P.G.S. VI B 3.
25 Visitation Report, July 27–31, 1892, GAR, P.G.S. VI A 5 b; PChr, unpaginated, [p. 1], PAG.
26 Schuster–Wildenauer 112.
27 Schriften III, 185–93.

CHAPTER SEVEN
AMONG CONFRERES

"There were quite a few things at that time that he did not like, because everything was not good."

No one lives for oneself, certainly not in a monastery. One lives with other people, their peculiarities, their rough spots, and with people one cannot choose, as everyone lives in a very restricted space. Add to all of this that Stanggassinger was lacking a separation between workspace and living space—something so necessary at times. As we can see from his notes, he experienced all of the problems of living in a monastery.

However, he also liked to be in the monastery with his confreres. He was silent about specific examples of his difficulties, about the moments of happiness that gave him courage, about confreres with whom he got along and about those with whom he did not. Until now, Stanggassinger's biographers to date have hardly written about the practical points of community life.

Instead, they paint the portrait of their "hero" on the golden ground of the monastery, living apart from the world and in brotherly harmony. The true background of his human environment is barely visible. And yet, no portrait of Kaspar

Stanggassinger can be complete without it. He, as with all of us, was not a lonely wanderer on his way to God. Rather he lived in a mesh of human relationships, and within the structures of his time. He was aware of tendencies and developments, and he participated in them. If hardly anything has been written about this background, it may have been in sensitive consideration of his confreres who were still alive. But also it could be that the biographers did not sufficiently recognize the importance of the human environment to the success or the failure of a Christian life.

Stanggassinger entered the southern German Redemptorist province at a time when there were strong inner tensions. The focal point of these tensions was Dürrnberg. As mentioned earlier, the province was in the process of being reconstituted after it had been banned. The time had come to rid the Redemptorists of an exaggerated strictness in pastoral work as well as in the life of the monastery. Most members of the province recognized and agreed that this shift in attitude was necessary. They did not agree about how far one should go with the reforms, and how quickly one should implement them.

The longer it took, the more the tensions grew. There was also a generational conflict, which became even more severe because of the absence of one generation. The older fathers, most of them over sixty years of age, who had joined before the ban, were opposed to the new, very young priests. These older men had joined the Congregation only after considerable reflection, usually with the goal to "save their soul." The young priests generally were fresh out of the juvenate when they joined. They sometimes lacked maturity and maybe some of them were pushed to join the monastery more than they should have been. Furthermore, they did not possess the self-discipline, which was occasionally—not always—characteristic of those whose vocation was realized at a more advanced age.

The reason the conflict took place in Dürrnberg was that the most talented of the younger (southern German) Redemptorists were there. Often these were called to be teachers while still studying. Based on their intellectual superiority over their older confreres, they had developed a solid self-confidence. They formed a strong "alliance" when it came to refuting rigorous views with respect to the education of youth. Unfortunately, their will to reform was undisciplined and all too often accompanied by immature behavior. What they achieved often turned into a radical confrontation.

At this point, Stanggassinger had a challenge.[1] Basically agreeing with the young reformers, he opposed their haste. Contrary to some of his young colleagues, he was a thoughtful and conscientious religious. His superiors valued his judgment. Hence he was able to help find a compromise in a difficult situation.

One who knew the situation said of Stanggassinger, "It seems he received his wisdom from the Holy Spirit; it allowed him to strike a good balance between 'spiritual' and 'secular' views in Dürrnberg."[2] Another confrere joined in, "He was certainly very wise, otherwise it would not have been possible to get by so well in Dürrnberg considering the great differences in character among its residents."[3] However, he did not always succeed as we can see from the following opinion, "He had his difficulties with some of his confreres."[4] Stanggassinger's function in these conflicts becomes evident from the words of a confrere who knew the situation in Dürrnberg during this time very well:

> There were quite a few things at that time that he did not like, because everything was not good. However, he uttered his criticism and his regrets tactfully and with the desire to turn mischief into the best situation for all. His position was a difficult one, spiked with thorns. He often felt this. For example, his friend, Father Schaumberger, called him a martyr who had to sacrifice himself.[5]

A better understanding of Stanggassinger's confreres and colleagues may clarify this. Among the fathers of the older generation, Father Joseph Wildgruber was the one with whom Stanggassinger principally dealt. When he became the director of the juvenate at age seventy, he was seen as a small, frail, often nervous, and sometimes depressed man with a strong, booming voice. Yet he could look back on his life in the Congregation as having been filled with work as a teacher, a leader of the juvenate, a well-liked missionary preacher and confessor.[6] Why the superiors chose him as director is unclear, since his sixty-year-old predecessor, Father Henry Stracke, was deemed no longer right for the position "because of his age."[7] Perhaps Father Wildgruber's appointment was meant only as an interim solution.

As a theology student in Dürrnberg in a photo from 1894–1895, Stanggassinger is in the second row from the bottom, the third from the left.

This is Dürrnberg, near Hallein, in the general vicinity of Salzburg, Austria. On the left is the pilgrimage shrine, in the middle is the former residence of the Redemptorists, and in the right-upper background is the preparatory seminary called "the Juvenate."

Stanggassinger's promotion to prefect and the great confidence that the provincial leadership had in him hinted at the fact that at least the provincial superior saw a future director in Stanggassinger.[8] Indeed, under Wildgruber, as mentioned earlier, some of the exaggerations had been done away with. There was no shortage of fathers who feared that a lax attitude would take hold at the juvenate under Wildgruber and Stanggassinger.

However, in general, things remained the same. It did not take long until the provincial, Anthony Schöpf, stated that the directors asked too much of the students. He preferred to see "all-around religious men, since they have just come in from the outside world and many are in their so-called rebellious years." He wrote to the leadership in Rome, "The young people who fail not out of ill-will, but because of childishness, who like to chat and joke—I will protect these from Wildgruber. He wants them to be serious and mature all the time. Later they, especially those who survive, will be very good."[9]

Alois Meier, who experienced Wildgruber from close-at-hand experience, came to a similar conclusion. He added, however, "If many had little good to say about Wildgruber's tenure as director of the juvenate in Dürrnberg, this can be explained and excused by his age. What the old man had to do was new and unusual for him. Father Provincial was far away. Thus he thought he had to rely solely on his own judgment alone. Since he did not care much for the advice of his older colleagues, at times there were many things that he decided to undertake, but at other times he neglected a lot that should have been done. He was later criticized for his decisions.[10] From the statements of Wildgruber's students, one gets the impression that they did not take their director very seriously. Whenever he lost control and had one of his temper tantrums, one could hear, "Quick, open the windows! Wildgruber is yelling."[11]

Stanggassinger also had run-ins with the director's anger from time to time. "When one of us juvenists did something wrong," one of the students remembers, "Father Wildgruber punished the innocent Father Stanggassinger with an outburst of anger."[12] It happened that Stanggassinger would say, "Today is one of those days when he really let me have it,"[13] but without a word of criticism or defense.[14] What else should he have possibly said? The director was obviously overextended.

Stanggassinger seemed more disturbed by Father Wildgruber's pettiness, according to one witness. For example he ordered Stanggassinger to ask his sisters not to visit so often. Or at times Stanggassinger saw from his window that Wildgruber sent his sisters away—and they left with tears in their eyes. However, the letter of the Rule was on the side of the director, and Stanggassinger remained silent.

What hurt him most was Wildgruber's lack of trust. Whenever Father Kaspar received a donation for the seminary, it did not suffice that he had to tell the director the amount, but he was ordered to bring the money to Wildgruber, who would then count it for exactness. While Stanggassinger did not say a word, one could see how much Wildgruber's actions hurt.[15]

In May 1898, Father Wildgruber was replaced by Father Aloys Kraft. Despite the fact that he was already sixty years of age, he was much more suited to the role. People said of him that he was a successful leader of the juvenate. Father Kraft, however, who was known as a fine, popular missionary, had never worked in the education of youth. Thus he focused on the general administration and spiritual leadership of the seminary. He even took over the weekly conference for the students, which previously Stanggassinger had been delivering. Everything that had to do with daily life in the seminary he left to the prefect and the other teachers, giving them plain guidelines on how they might fulfill their roles.

Stanggassinger was closer to Father Kraft than to Wildgruber and also chose Kraft as his confessor. This trust was mutual. While not customary at the time, the director also addressed Stanggassinger by his first name.[16] Thus, Kraft was one of the two confreres who were to be affected deeply by Stanggassinger's death. Father Wildgruber, however, said of Stanggassinger later, "He led the juvenate under the guidance of the Father Director in a sensible and prudent way. The juvenists liked him and had full confidence in him." Father Wildgruber is also reported to have said, "Oh, Father Stanggassinger! He had to put up with a lot from the young fathers."[17]

Who were these young fathers who were teaching together with Stanggassinger in Dürrnberg? Here we introduce a few and comment on them. There were three highly talented young fathers: Frederick Häfele, Francis Forner, and Dennis Hubbauer. They were the first of the Dürrnberg high school students who passed the general Bavarian university qualifying examination, thanks to their talent. When Stanggassinger took his vows, they were invested in the Redemptorist habit. While they were still students, they started teaching at the high school.[18]

The most able among these "student lecturers" was without a doubt Häfele, who even prepared his fellow novices for the qualifying examination. He enjoyed a good reputation, especially in the higher grades, because of his pedagogical gifts and his quiet and friendly demeanor. To his superiors he seemed irreplaceable. It must have hit them hard when he informed them in August 1897 that he wanted to leave the Congregation and become a diocesan priest. Because various superiors urged him to stay, (especially Father Karl Dilgskron, who came to Dürrnberg as a Roman Visitator in September 1897), Häfele stayed—but only for one more year. Shortly after his ordination he requested his dispensation from vows and left the Redemptorists.[19] When one digs deeper regarding his departure, we find that he could no longer stand the unkindness and infighting among the young fathers, nor their secular outlook. Such religious, he told his students, are a "scandal." They were turning the seminary into a den of thieves. He thought, "Either a true religious or none at all."[20]

However, Häfele may have had another reason to leave as

he obviously dreamt of a scholarly career. How else can we understand Stanggassinger's comments on his leaving, "The Redemptorists have no use for overly intelligent men, those who always study, even during prayer time."[21] He wrote in his notebook shortly after Häfele departed, "What a calamity to take off the holy habit and to return to the world. But isn't it equally sad to wear the holy habit and yet to live as if you were in the outside world?"[22] Of course, Häfele suffered bitter disappointment. He was not accepted for higher studies in the diocese of Rottenburg. Since he did not study theology at Tübingen, he finally had to be content that the Württemberg government allowed him, after a long waiting period, to occupy a pastoral post. He spent the rest of his life in small country parishes. His community appreciated him because of his knowledge and deep piety, but also because of his forthright position during the Nazi years. Even today, people speak with enthusiasm of his teaching of catechism. Häfele died as pastor of Ingerkirchen near Biberach on July 1, 1948.[23]

Francis Forner was not less talented than Häfele. He came to Dürrnberg in the summer of 1896 and there took on the sixth level's Latin course. After teaching for two years and his subsequent ordination, he was sent on an interim basis to the new house of study in Deggendorf on the Danube. In the autumn of 1900, along with another father, and at the wish of the Redemptorist Generalate, Father Forner began his studies in philology in Munich. Soon, however, some rumors about the two priests reached Gars and Rome; there was concern about their perseverance as Redemptorists and suspicion about their orthodoxy. Influential senior fathers urged their return from Munich. However, Forner preempted this decision. He joined the diocese of Munich-Freising[24] and later became pastor in Velden on the Vils, where he died in 1938.[25]

What stands out, contrary to other contemporary students, is that hardly anything can be located regarding Forner in the time he spent at Dürrnberg. The reason for this may be that he obviously was not one of the vociferous reformists. Stanggassinger's papers likewise are silent about Forner.

Dennis Hubbauer was Stanggassinger's colleague for a longer period than were Häfele and Forner. He had begun his Dürrnberg studies on July 25, 1896, and was known as a genius in mathematics. There he became a teacher of mathematics, physics, and mineralogy, and remained in that role after the transfer of the juvenate to Gars. Hubbauer was more outspoken than Häfele and Forner. Although he was considered "observant of the Rules," he did not shy away from disputes with his superiors. His wish to study mathematics in Munich was denied.[26] With the permission of his superiors he later lived outside the monastery. He was an assistant pastor in the parish of his colleague Forner and was known to have developed into an eccentric individual.[27] As was said of Forner, we know nothing of how he interacted with Stanggassinger.[28]

Another man, Father Sebastian Seidl, created trouble in the juvenate. He was among the first Bavarians to join the seminary. As a student, he already stood out by what he termed "southern Bavarian straightforwardness," which, however, was really nothing but a good deal of bawdy and crass behavior. He wanted to become a pastor, a difference in attitude from what most of his colleagues wanted. But he was ready "to obey and be just a teacher." As a good musician, and as the leader of the seminary choir, he seemed indispensable in Dürrnberg. The superiors, however, were not unaware that he had habits that created difficulties for his confreres as well as his students. They complained that he was full of himself and that he possessed little religious spirit. Nevertheless, they hoped that this would change with time, since he had good intentions.[29] His students judged him more sharply. They were afraid of his "reign of terror." He had, they said, developed in the years 1895 to 1898 a kind of "control-by-terror of all the juvenists and even some of the fathers." Since Father Joseph Wildgruber was sick most of the time, Seidl could generally do whatever he pleased in the "lower house." This gave the appearance that Father Seidl was the director of the juvenate and that he could bully the juvenists however he pleased.

There is no doubt that he had good intentions. Having suffered under Father Henry Stracke's administration, Seidl kept pointing out that the "saints of the juvenate," who had followed orders blindly, did not succeed in their later lives. He could not suffer the do-gooders and young conformists. He preferred rough youngsters, of whom he wanted to be the roughest, and he constantly used expressions like "coward, rascal, and stupid." If one of them was attacked, he would shout, "Go ahead, fight back! Don't let them do this to you!" A scuffle might have erupted, and then he was right in the middle of it.

However well-intentioned, sometimes his so-called "psychology" went too far. For example, he often slapped students. He scolded shy students until they cried. One such was Pelag Sauter, who today is revered as a saint in Brazil. Sometimes he stared at a student in the auditorium for half an hour and then told him, "You're a good-for-nothing!"[30]

Finally in 1898, Seidl was removed from Dürrnberg, and not only because of his educational methods. He had simply granted himself permissions that in earlier times would have caused his dismissal. Even after his removal, there was reason for complaint. However, since he was the "best of preachers," there had been a reluctance to remove him. He also kept promising that he would improve. Not the least reason for this reluctance was he had made a name for himself by writing a defense of Saint Alphonsus. Therefore, the superiors had more patience with him than he would have had for himself. In May 1902 he left the Congregation. In 1927, only fifty-five years of age, he died as a pastor in the Regensburg diocese.[31]

Seidl had been ordained on the same day as Stanggassinger and assisted with his classmate's first Mass in Berchtesgaden.[32] He had little contact with Stanggassinger in Dürrnberg, since Stanggassinger was in the "upper house" with the other juvenists. However, Seidl was angry that Stanggassinger, and not he, had been made consultor to the rector. He also seems to have tried to extend his influence to the "upper house" and sometimes the older students complained to Stanggassinger about Seidl. Then Stanggassinger could say, "He will push so far that no one will stand it any longer." He admonished the students not to provoke Seidl: "He is a lion. It is better not to provoke him."[33] Once when Seidl slapped a student, Stanggassinger confronted him.[34] On another occasion he seems not to have found the courage. Stanggassinger's biographer, Father Joseph Schuster, told the story:

> The choir members were allowed to go on an outing with Father Seidl. As if on a power trip, he excluded four of them. At home they locked their door and made a tremendous ruckus. Stanggassinger knocked on their door, "Why the noise?" "We were treated unjustly," [one said]. Stanggassinger did not punish them; he believed they were justified in their complaints. Blood rushed to his head and he left the room. Should he not have taken the students' side and put Seidl in his place?[35]

Completely different than Seidl was Father Karl Baudenbacher, who was also one of the first Bavarian juvenists. During the whole time that Stanggassinger was active in Dürrnberg, Baudenbacher was his colleague and lived next to him in the "upper house." Even if Stanggassinger appeared too pious to him at times, he looked up to him and he valued his opinion. However, Baudenbacher was a rather unhappy person. For early in his youth to the end of his life, he was plagued by mental suffering. Most of his later life, he spent outside of the monastery, mostly in different sanatoria.

Baudenbacher immersed himself with all of his soul in the Congregation, despite knowing that he was not made for life in the Congregation. His superiors did not know what to do with this "poor, mysterious man." They complained about his "childlike behavior," his "craziness," and his "disobedience." Even later, when he had made a name for himself as a religious writer, he was much more respected outside of the Congregation than by his confreres.[36] (Besides numerous magazine articles, he wrote twenty popular books dealing with religious, pedagogical, and historical subjects).

As long as Baudenbacher was in Dürrnberg he suffered under Father Seidl, since he was Seidl's best example of a "saint of the juvenate." "As a juvenist he could not be pious enough! And what has happened to him now?" One of the students of Dürrnberg wrote, "Father Seidl showed no love, I am tempted to say he showed hatred towards Father Baudenbacher, so much so that it caused general concern." Another student wrote: "General annoyance was caused by the lack of fraternal consideration displayed by Father Seidl vis-à-vis Father Baudenbacher. He used any and all occasions to assail Father Baudenbacher."[37]

It must have been especially important to Baudenbacher to be understood by Stanggassinger. He went to him when he had insurmountable difficulties with his class. This may have been the reason that Baudenbacher's class did exceptionally well on the occasion of the next school visit by the provincial, Father Schöpf.[38]

Baudenbacher would never forget his last meeting with

Stanggassinger shortly before Stanggassinger's death. As so often before, he had come out of his superior's room with tears in his eyes. Stanggassinger saw him and comforted him. Baudenbacher also remembers that Stanggassinger paid him a visit when he was sick. "I do not need to tell you about patience and suffering," he said, "you are a priest yourself. You know what to do."[39] Shortly before his death in 1936, Baudenbacher made a glowing report about Stanggassinger. It is notably different than some of the praise-filled statements during the process of beatification. Nowhere else does Stanggassinger's humanity stand out so clearly as in the account by Baudenbacher.[40]

From our files another Redemptorist stands out quite brilliantly who, more than anyone else, represented the new beginning of the Bavarian province around the turn of the century. We refer to Father Alois Meier. He was one of the first Bavarian juvenists, a man with exceptional talents and literary gifts, an excellent Latin scholar and a passionate historian of the Congregation. The reform-oriented forces in the southern German province gathered around him. While he may have aimed too high at times, he never looked for personal advantages, as did Seidl and Hubbauer. He demanded a turning away from the letter and a move toward the spirit of the Rules of the Congregation. In pursuit of such change he was inspired by his work as provincial archivist. This role afforded him insight into the various aberrations by former Redemptorist superiors and their subjects who obeyed all too blindly.[41]

Alois Meier was a teacher in Dürrnberg with Stanggassinger in 1895–1896 and 1898–1899. What did Meier think of Stanggassinger? The best answer is certainly the biography of Stanggassinger, which he published for the first time in 1902, and which contributed greatly to keep Stanggassinger's memory alive. Meier's reaction to Stanggassinger's death speaks for itself: Meier wept aloud. He was inconsolable and insisted on holding the hand of the deceased.[42] He kept Stanggassinger's prayer books and writings and guarded them like relics, even if he did not believe Stanggassinger would be beatified.[43]

Despite this, some doubted Meier's good relationship with Stanggassinger.[44] This may have been because Meier was often judged by his rough exterior, and confreres could not see a friendship between the two. Meier underlines in his biography that Stanggassinger was "very conservative in his positions," which differed from Meier's attitude. However, he adds, "he always had sound judgment."[45] That was important to Meier, whose own heavy criticism was feared by others.

At the end of this overview of Stanggassinger's confreres we have to turn to one man who did not stand out like the others: Father John Baptist Schaumberger. Like Stanggassinger, he lived in the "upper house" and he was considered Stanggassinger's friend.[46] He really did not belong to the "young fathers." When he entered the monastery in 1894, he was almost forty-five years old. He had been a pastor in the Regensburg diocese. Despite his poor eyesight, which forced him to interrupt his high school education, he was the best student not only in high school, but also at the university level. Later, among forty-nine priest candidates he wrote the best examination. Schaumberger was ordained in 1874 and since 1876 wanted to become a Redemptorist. (While Redemptorist priests were exiled from Bavaria, he was both a sought-out confessor and spiritual director for the Redemptorist Brothers who stayed behind at former Redemptorist houses). In 1883 he began his novitiate but was not allowed to continue because of his eyesight. He finally professed his vows in 1894 and soon became a teacher in Dürrnberg, where he taught only the higher classes. However, he did not know how to transmit his great knowledge. Still, what he lacked in pedagogical ability he made up for in pastoral fervor. Most seminarians appreciated him as a preacher and as a confessor. At recreation time he proved to be quite joyful, and he also liked to make up humorous lines of verse. He was exemplary in his piety and his helpfulness.

Father Schaumberger's later life took an unusual course. In 1903, at the age of fifty-four, he volunteered for the Brazilian mission. Within a short time he was speaking fluent Portuguese, and he also wrote spiritual songs in that language. He likewise heard the confessions of many pilgrims who came to the Marian Shrine of Aparecida. He taught high school students and even theology students, and he wrote a short Latin grammar course for the Brazilian students in Portuguese. During all of this time he was almost blind. On March 31, 1908, he was shot to death by a fanatic on a street in Sao Paolo, for the simple reason that he was a priest.[47]

We could list some other confreres, such as Father Kirchmeier who taught mathematics in the juvenate before Hubbauer, and who went to Brazil in 1897. There he pioneered and persevered as a long-serving director of the juvenate. Later he was a community rector, and then was superior of the entire foreign mission. He died, advanced in years, on June 13, 1958.[48] Of those Dürrnberg confreres whom we have met, no fewer than three left the Congregation completely, and two later lived outside of their religious communities. This in some way confirms what we cited at the beginning of this chapter: "[Stanggassinger] was certainly very wise, otherwise it would not have been possible to get by so well in Dürrnberg considering the great differences in character among its residents." This is also confirmed by the details we have described. Even if we would like to know more about the relationship between Stanggassinger and his confreres, these brief descriptions do shine a light on Stanggassinger himself; even in Dürrnberg he stayed true to his principle to respect the opinions of others[49] as he followed his own path.

ENDNOTES

1 Weiss 761–83.
2 Zeugnisse 79.
3 Causa Mon. 412.
4 Causa Mon. 350.
5 Zeugnisse 201.
6 Wildgruber personnel file, PAG.
7 Visitation Report by Schöpf, August 26–September 10, 1894, GAR, P.G.S. VI A 5 c.
8 Cf. Visitation Report, November 30–December 2, 1898, GAR, P.G.S. VI 5 a.
9 Visitation Report 1896, GAR, P.G.S. VI B 2.

10 *Meier*, Commentarii 1908, 154.
11 Summarium, 207.
12 Causa Mon. 366; cf. ibid., 141, 333, 350, 380.
13 Causa Mon. 350, 363.
14 Causa Mon. 363.
15 Zeugnisse 93.
16 Visitation Report, November 30–December 2, 1898, GAR, P.G.S. VI B 5a; Suppl. 74; Zeugnisse 201, Summarium 257.
17 Zeugnisse 93.
18 Untergehrer, passim.
19 Dilgskron to Generalate, August 5, 1897; September 20, 1897, GAR, P.G.S. VI B 3; Baumgartner to Generalate, December 9, 1897, GAR, P.G.S. IV C 2.
20 A. Khuon to Generalate, December 19, 1898; J. Zartmann to Generalate December 21, 1898, GAR, P.G.S. VII A 1.
21 Causa Mon. 277; Zeugnisse 24f.
22 Schriften II/2, 134.
23 General catalog of members of Upper German Province, PAG.
24 PChr, passim, PAG; Unterkehrer, passim; Weiss passim.
25 Information in Parish Office, Velden/Vils.
26 Visitation Report, GAR, P.G.S. VI; PChr, passim; Untergehrer, passim.
27 Information Parish Office, Velden/Vils.
28 Causa Mon. 389; Summarium 234.
29 Visitation Report GAR, P.G.S. VI.
30 A. Khuon, J. Heinrich, J. Zartman to Generalate; December 19–21, 1898, GAR, P.G.S. VII A 1; Memo Gebhard Heni to Wildenauer, StAG.
31 Correspondence of the Upper German Province to the Generalate, GAR, P.G.S., VIff; StAG; Weiss, passim.
32 Seidl to Schöpf, June 28, 1895, StAG.
33 A. Khuon, J. Heinrich, J. Zartmann to Generalate December 19–21, 1898, GAR, P.G.S. VII A 1.
34 Summarium 165.
35 Causa Mon. 335f.; Schuster–Wildenauer 120ff.; also, memo. by Heni, StAG (According to Heni, who was one of the noise makers, Stanggassinger had laughed at the noise).
36 Baudenbacher personnel file, PAG; Visitation Reports and correspondence with Generalate, GAR, P.G.S. VIff.
37 Karl Dilgskron to Generalate, September 20, 1897, GAR, P.G.S. VI B 3; A. Khuon, J. Heinrich, J. Zartmann (see note 30).
38 Summarium 205; Visitation Report 1896, GAR, P.G.S. VI B 2.
39 Zeugnisse 300f.
40 Zeugnisse 200–209.
41 Meier personnel file, PAG; Correspondence with Generalate, GAR, P.G.S. VIff.; Weiss 754–8.
42 Zeugnisse 208.
43 *Meier*, passim.

44 Summarium 234.
45 *Meier* 206.
46 Visitation Report 1898, GAR, P.G.S. VI B 5 a; Zeugnisse 201.
47 *Meier*, Commentarii 1911, 177–82; K. Baudenbacher, *P. Johann Baptist Schaumberger, CSsR, ein Mariensänger* (Regensburg 1909).
48 *Catalogi CSsR,* GAR; "Cronica da Comunidade Redentorista de Aparecida 1892–1894," passim; "Cronica da Campinas de Goias, Aparecida 1982," passim.
49 Cf. Zeugnisse 201.

CHAPTER EIGHT
THE EVERYDAY LIFE OF A PREFECT

"He did not have to scold us.
We felt tremendously guilty to hurt
such a generous person."

How did Stanggassinger's students see their prefect? Only trivial details—extremely important for young students—were remembered. These details, however unimportant they may be, clearly show that Stanggassinger did not stop at good intentions when he wrote in his notebook that he wants to be "a servant to all."[1]

There is some basis for his students' declarations about their teacher: "We all liked him because of his good heart and his charity toward us."[2] Or, "despite the fact that he was overworked, his door was always open. As a dear father, he earned everyone's trust, and everyone came to see him. They lined up outside his door. He only smiled about it, saying, 'this goes on all day.'"[3]

One of his students wrote, "Father Stanggassinger was—and I cannot use any different words—our father for the body and soul. He loved the juvenate and the juvenists with all his heart. He said, 'the juvenate is hearth and home to me.' When the other teachers went on vacations to other monasteries, he always stayed with us."[4] Another commented, "Everyone wanted to walk with him when we took a walk. He walked with us as a father does with his children, and we hung onto him like children do with their father."[5]

Stanggassinger knew how to win the hearts of all of his students, even the difficult ones. "He was unusually objective. He did not know any prejudice," one of his students wrote. And another, "He was of rare impartiality.[6] He showed great charity to those who were naturally slow."[7]

To such fundamental opinions we can add the anecdotes describing Stanggassinger in everyday situations: in his leisure time, when hiking, when he had to discipline, when he had to care for sick students, when teaching, when he taught religion. In these situations, one cannot find any long-term pretense and can only see what he was really like. How was Stanggassinger in the eyes of his students?

Stanggassinger did everything, the students said, so that their leisure time was varied and relaxing. He had a simple recipe: "Be happy, sing, play."[8] He did not think it beneficial for students to "laze around" or "brood." "I always worry about those who are always sad," he used to say.[9] He was their best example and liked to laugh heartily, especially when he recited something called the Sermons of Abraham to Saint Clara.[10] He was also fond of singing funny songs.[11]

So it is not surprising how a student remembered and wrote: "What impressed us most about him was his naturalness. He was always jovial and in good spirits, especially when he did the dishes after a meal. It was then he told interesting and funny stories. We liked to help him at this task."[12]

Stanggassinger was a friend of song and music.[13] He tried in vain to have the students provided with a choice between the more serious piano music and the lighter music for brass instruments.[14] He also liked sports and games. It was due to his efforts that parallel bars and other gymnastic equipment were purchased.[15] Without too much theory he practiced a holistic education that included education of the body. This brought on considerable resistance from some members in the Congregation. Stanggassinger showed new games to his students, and to the bemusement of his colleagues, he often demonstrated these games himself, in spite of the Redemptorist Rule that then forbade any kind of game.[16] The prefect almost always accompanied his students on their walks. While other teachers tried to avoid doing this, he always made the time. Especially during periods of vacation, when the students had to stay at the minor seminary (over his objections), he took a number of trips with them.

He was always concerned that the students had enough to eat and drink. No one was to go hungry. He also believed that "on holidays the body should be included in the celebration."[17] He often gave some of his own portions of food to the students. They could not understand how anyone could live off so little.[18]

One excursion especially remained in his students' memories: the "hike to the waterfall at Golling. They did not plan to walk that far. But, by accident, they came so close to the waterfall that they could hear it. It could be only a half-hour at the most, one of the students said, so why not continue on? The prefect agreed.

Finally, after three hours, they arrived at the waterfall. They were hungry and thirsty. But Stanggassinger did not have a penny on him. What was more, he did not have the director's permission. He did something that today seems obvious. At the time it was unusual. He decided to go into a pub and ask for credit. How he justified this to his superior, Joseph Wildgruber, we do not know. One student later said that he received a severe punishment.[19]

Stanggassinger did not hand out punishments lightly. His students said that he "never did hit anyone, and he never humiliated anyone in front of others. He asked the students to his room and talked things out. Usually this was the only punishment.[20]

"If he had to dole out punishment, he discussed the sense of punishment with the guilty one. He never dwelt on someone's previous mistakes. Often he said, 'It hurts me when I have to punish.'"[21] Therefore, it is easy to understand when his students reported, "He did not have to scold us. We felt tremendously guilty to hurt such a generous man."[22] When Stanggassinger once punished a student wrongly, he was not shy about admitting the mistake. "He knelt down before me and said that he had been unjust and he asked me for forgiveness. I was so moved that I had tears streaming down my cheeks."[23]

There were some, of course, who saw this as a weakness; it was the same judgment made when he did not just give orders but politely asked his students to do something: "May I ask you ..." Later, though, they changed their views. They recognized that this was not weakness, even if it was unusual.[24] "At first sight, one thought that he was afraid of the juvenists," one of his students wrote, "especially if one was accustomed to Father Wildgruber's approach. Or, that of Father Stracke before him. Both of them employed rough means. Stanggassinger's gracious, low-key approach was in sharp contrast to them. However, it was not out of fear, it was his system. He wanted to educate graciously and peacefully."[25]

Stanggassinger was especially concerned about his sick students, but not the hypochondriacs. Whoever was really sick was in good hands with him. "He often came to the infirmary to see how they were, to comfort them, to help them feel good and to make sure they were well-cared-for.... No father could have done it better." The sick students were not the only ones to become talkative and confide their innermost concerns to the prefect. The teacher sometimes also "removed the veil from the secrets of his own inner life." He told them how it was sometimes difficult for him at the seminary and how he coped with his problems with God's help.[26]

There was one incident that none of the pupils ever forgot. Their colleague, Alois Fischbach, had fallen ill with tuberculosis in 1898. Stanggassinger stayed at his bed until his death. The others were almost jealous. They believed that someone who was accompanied by Stanggassinger to his death would be immediately accepted into heaven.[27]

Not only as their prefect, but also as their teacher, Stanggassinger remained strongly imbedded in their memories. He was an effective teacher. "He showed such patience in the schoolroom that we often asked ourselves how he could stand it without getting angry." What came into play here was that he himself had had difficulties in school. Hence, he could explain things very well.[28] Moreover, Stanggassinger took his task as a teacher very seriously. When he took over the fourth level, he was assigned to teach Greek—besides religion, German, and Latin.[29] In any case, he prepared himself with intensity. Not a day passed that he did not collect his students' notebooks. Late at night, when the others were asleep, he corrected the homework, and then completed some other written work.[30] It was no surprise, then, that a brother in the community one morning found him sleeping on the floor. He had fallen asleep as he prayed Compline, which he ordinarily did on his knees.[31] "Of course," Stanggassinger admitted one day, "I would prefer to read sacred Scripture than this dry stuff over and over again. But God gave me this job to do, and I will correct homework as long as I have time. I will do my best for my students so that they can have a good future."[32]

Stanggassinger's religion lessons remained unforgettable. He prepared them the best. He told his students, "I am happy that I can instruct so many young students in religion."[33] The students, however, experienced lessons that not only provided knowledge but included a testament of the deepest faith.[34] "Before I came to Dürrnberg, I had two religion teachers," one student wrote, "neither of whom helped us much in our faith. I was moved when I had my first lesson with Father Stanggassinger. It was clearly obvious that he was fully part of what he said."[35]

There are two episodes that belong here, near the end of this description of Stanggassinger as a teacher. Both of them show in their own way that his superiors did well to give Stanggassinger the task of educating the youth of the Congregation. Once, a student looked up some "immodest vocabulary" and had been denounced to Stanggassinger. According to the custom of the time, the student was to expect a large punishment. It was otherwise with Stanggassinger, as the responsible party himself narrated: "Father Stanggassinger asked me if I had anything on my conscience. I knew immediately what he was referring to and I admitted that out of curiosity I had looked up certain words in the dictionary. 'Be glad,' he said, 'that you do not have to learn such difficult expressions.' However, if I had a difficult time with my conscience, I could go to confession with Father Schaumberger. All was OK again, and Father Stanggassinger did not hold a grudge. I did not have the impression that I had been treated unjustly. I thought that he fully understood me."[36]

Here we can see one of Stanggassinger's most important qualities: he sought to understand his students. He did so in cases like the one just described, in which he resolved problems that adolescents normally encounter. But he also tried to discern the best remedy when he noticed deeper psychological distress in youngsters, for example, if they had no self-confidence, or suffered from scruples. He tried to make them smile with small jokes. When they were his penitents, he tried to lead them from their fears to happiness. Once, however, with an especially difficult case, only the following phrase worked, "Now I am fresh out of ideas. Are you really that stupid?" The one who heard this from Stanggassinger was thankful for it the rest of his life.[37]

Another student reported the following episode. It was the usual practice in the seminary that the students' letters were read by their directors. This student noticed that Stanggassinger gave the older students their letters unopened. He asked him why he did that. The prefect answered that he believed that someone who had spent so much time in the seminary had earned some trust.[38]

In many other reports we find evidence of Stanggassinger's same basic attitude of trust.

He is said to have had "great respect and reverence" for his students.[39] Today we would say that he took them seriously. They were not educational objects that he talked at. He saw as them living human beings who were loved by God, personalities with their own intellect and their own will, as he had read in Doupanloup's writings. He was convinced of this and acted accordingly. However, there was something more than ordinary human maturity at work in Stanggassinger. In addition, the legacy of God's love was alive in him—that love that took us humans very seriously.

ENDNOTES

1 Schriften II/2, 134.
2 Causa Mon. 272.
3 Supp. 43; Zeugnisse 92.
4 Zeugnisse 103.
5 Causa Mon. 367.
6 Summarium 168, 174.
7 Causa Mon. 267f.; Zeugnisse 156.
8 Cf. Suppl. 20.
9 Suppl. 74; Zeugnisse 109; cf Schriften III, 296.
10 Causa Mon. 428; Summarium 210.
11 Causa Mon. 281.
12 Zeugnisse 157; Causa Mon. 281.
13 Causa Mon. 276.
14 Juvenate teachers to Generalate, July 5, 1900, GAR, P.G.S. VII A 2.
15 Summarium 206; cf. Schriften III, 297.
16 Suppl. 73; Zeugnisse 109, 203.
17 Zeugnisse 25.
18 Causa Mon. 338, 429.
19 Zeugnisse 27f.; Summarium 197.
20 Causa Mon. 339; Suppl. 78.
21 Zeugnisse 105.
22 Suppl. 43.
23 Summarium 201; cf. Causa Mon. 274f., 397.
24 Causa Mon. 430; Zeugnisse 195.
25 Zeugnisse 190f.; Causa Mon. 280.
26 Causa Mon. 279; Zeugnisse 190, 210; Summarium 206.
27 Zeugnisse 210f.; Summarium 206, 208.
28 Suppl. 60.
29 Causa Mon. 268.
30 Summarium 267; Zeugnisse 108.
31 Summarium 273.
32 Suppl. 75.
33 Suppl. 59.
34 Causa Mon. 273; Summarium 209.
35 Suppl. 59; Zeugnisse 183.
36 Summarium 176.
37 Zeugnisse 199.
38 Causa Mon. 285.
39 Zeugnisse 104; Suppl. 73.

CHAPTER NINE

A STAR THAT LEADS TO CHRIST

"All of you who know and love God,
understand what I say:
God is everything, we are nothing."

Stanggassinger's students celebrated his name day. After the director had refused permission for the celebration, they got permission from the provincial. They praised the prefect in a poem as a "star that leads to Christ." (It was the day of the Three Wise Men.) Clearly, he was embarrassed by such praise as one could see from his face.[1] However, it was well put. As much as Stanggassinger tried to make mature and balanced people of his students, it was more important to him that faith in God and Jesus Christ become the deepest truth of their lives. This truth reigned, regardless of whether after their exams they did become priests and members of the Congregation, or they did not.

How Stanggassinger understood his duty to educate is recorded in the religious conferences and retreat talks he presented to his students. They are available in a four hundred-page typewritten volume.[2] One would be disappointed in looking for an original idea. Rather, one finds something much more important: the transmission of his own religious experience. We notice three things:

First: There is no noncommittal religious drivel. Leading carefully and with a full understanding of human weakness, he clearly calls for decision-making. Time and again, Stanggassinger returns to the Ignatian image of the banners of two armies, and which of these a man must choose. Well known to his students, there is also the recurring image of "Hercules at the crossroads."[3]

Second: The same basic religious experience runs like a red thread through his talks and also in his private notes: without God's grace, all our actions amount to nothing, and one who is touched by God must prove himself in everyday life through his actions.

Third (and here Stanggassinger echoes part of his own life experience): He presents a recipe for living. "Do not rush anything!" "Take one step after another!" (This phrase was also on a piece of paper on his desk.)[4] To do what the day demands.

If we now turn to the individual topics of Stanggassinger's spiritual conferences, we are surprised. The man, whose life *was* lived faith, talks in detail about education toward "humanity." This is the goal of studying and means nothing else but the "training of the whole human being, the harmonic unfolding of his powers and abilities, the intellect through the sciences, the will through strength of character, the heart through virtue." Any kind of halfhearted education and know-it-all pretense is evil. It is important to learn how to think. It is in this context that Stanggassinger studied Latin, Greek, and "the classics." If the study of the ancient languages helped in clear thinking, reading the classics provided understanding of "the light and the dark side of the greatness, blossoming, and decay of the ancient world." He liked the expression of the Church Fathers that declared that "the seeds of truth" had also been sown among the heathens. Everything that is human, noble and good has divinity in it. Of course, Stanggassinger did not stop there. In Christianity, "humanity became truth." Therefore, "the true ideal of man shall not be Greek or Roman, but Christ."[5]

Stanggassinger left no doubt about what is most important. "Let us rise above everyday thinking," he called out to his students. "Let us not contemplate only the height of a mountain, the depth of the sea, or the rules of grammar and the formulae of mathematics; let us think about ourselves, about our dignity."[6]

"One must get to know oneself," he told them. "This learning is more important than any other kind of learning. This learning lasts a lifetime." Stanggassinger continued, "Without self-awareness one cannot turn inward. Everything remains superficial. Nothing has any depth."[7] But how does one achieve true self-awareness? "Only he who has been illumined by God, only he who prays can become aware of himself."[8] For, as a Christian, true self-awareness means to know that his inner life is the grace of God, even God himself. It also means that we know that we carry this treasure in an earthly vessel. It is true for a Christian that he is a new creation in Christ, through his grace. "Grace is divine life which we receive from the heart of God; so that it is no longer we who live, but Jesus lives in us."[9] Stanggassinger says that grace is the "starting point" of our life and also its "destination."[10] Or, (instead of grace), should he rather say: "God is both?"

Stanggassinger did say so, and he gave his life as witness to this truth. "All of you who know and love God, understand and feel what I say: God is everything, we are nothing."[11] To love God more and more is the only rewarding goal in life.... To reach this goal, we must walk "the way of purification," to take off the old human being and to fight the spiritual fight.

Stanggassinger's source was Lorenzo Scupoli, whose book, *The Spiritual Combat*, he quoted repeatedly in this context. Increasingly, he referred to the founder of his Congregation, Saint Alphonsus Liguori, whose writings Stanggassinger studied in meditation. One of the most concise analogies of the mystical teacher, Saint John of the Cross, reached him by way of Saint Alphonsus. He transmitted this analogy to his students. It describes a bird that cannot fly, even if the line that ties him is very slight. On the way to God, this line, the last tie, must be broken in order for the soul to run joyfully toward God. The goal is worth every effort.[12]

His conferences held a second classical analogy from

mystical literature. He also took this example from Saint Alphonsus Liguori: the image of constructing a house. The larger the house should be, the deeper the foundation must be.[13] This can be achieved only through tireless work. "No false self-commitment," he told his students. Do not rest too early! Stanggassinger reminded them of an experience he had while hiking in the mountains. He thought he was high up. Only when he had reached the next height could he see the mountain peaks reaching into the sky. Then he had to keep on going.[14] Don't get lazy! Is it not Saint Alphonsus Liguori who says that the love of God lessens when one does only what he has to do?[15]

Stanggassinger often returned to the idea of lukewarmness. Once he was listing the errors of a tepid Christian and he suddenly interrupted himself: "I do not want to hurt you with this portrayal of tepidity; I do not think that even one of you leads such a life. I want to admonish and warn you, in all kindness and love."[16]

However, Stanggassinger asked a lot from his students. It was nothing less than "to follow Jesus and in this way to become holy."[17] Because "it is not the place nor the climate that make a saint, but the grace of the Holy Spirit, which blows where it wills."[18] How does one become holy? In answering this question Stanggassinger was something of an expert. "To be holy," he said in the spirit of Saint Alphonsus, "is nothing but to fulfill the will of God and to live it the way he wants it."[19] And what does God want? "I do not want that those who follow me have worse clothing and accommodation, worse food and drink than I. I ask only that they follow me."[20] This means concretely, "The boy Jesus swept the house, washed the dishes, brought in wood and water... this is what the Son of God did. One is never small when one tries to walk in the footsteps of God."[21]

Thus the point is to do well that which one does anyway. "To clean a dish in obedience, to sweep a room, to study diligently is great before God; to go around the world in disobedience, even preaching the Gospel, means nothing before God."[22]

"If one does the task on hand badly or halfheartedly or not at all, one does not reach the point where one can achieve the great things one aims for. Everything stays as only an image in the mind."[23]

At least as important, if not more important than the fulfillment of daily chores, there is the matter of prayer. "Pray, pray, pray," Stanggassinger stated in many sermons. And in another sermon, we find the phrases, "Pray always! The heart's flight to God is not tied to certain times, places and patterns."[24] Stanggassinger insisted, "Piety is not only for children and devout souls. Everyone should and must be pious." And, at a different time, "It is not a rule to celebrate the series of Sundays in honor of Saint Aloysius. It is well-meaning advice. Something else, however, is a rule: that you must be pious like Saint Aloysius!" And even with prayer he stated: do not rush things. "I do not ask that you should be in the chapel all day or that you become praying fanatics. Far from it! But that you visit the house chapel frequently during your vacations and that you pray the Way of the Cross, or another prayer, is not asking too much."[25] For Stanggassinger, the pinnacle of prayer was the Mass, since our praying and self-sacrificing becomes included there in the sacrificial death of Jesus. To celebrate Mass with devotion means to join in the sacrifice. Stanggassinger said, "The Mass is the center of the Christian religion, the heart of devotion, the soul of piety. It is the highest good, the best treasure, the most magnificent riches, the greatest joy, the most sacred domain of holiness in the Catholic Church."[26]

While we do not always know what sources Stanggassinger may have consulted, the material he gave to his students—at a time when there were few outstanding theologians—is of high quality. It is even more: it is evidence of a deep faith. "It is on the cross that the eternal fountain of redemption was opened. At the altar it streams ever forth into the hearts of people. From the altar God distributes the fullness of heaven and eternal life to all who desire it. Go there! This is the tree of life! The Mass is the heart of all Christian life. All life comes from the heart."[27]

Stanggassinger was unusual for his time in urging people to frequent Communion. Even more unusual is his wish that "holy Communion should, whenever possible, be administered during Mass."[28] Half a century would pass until this wish of his became a reality.

However much Stanggassinger's teaching put the inner life—devotion to God—at the center, he did not forget to remind his students that God would judge our actions by how we deal with our fellow human beings. Love for God and love for others go hand in hand. "Write this principle in your heart: no half commitment to God, no lack of love towards your neighbor, and no softness towards oneself!"[29]

A few days before his death he was repeating to his students how important "kindness and charity" are: "If you want God's blessing, the love and respect of the people, and peace in your heart, then run away from anger!" With Saint Bernard he admonished them to put love higher even than intelligence and knowledge which make for self-absorption, leading a person to "fight stubbornly, inconsiderately, and bitterly the opinions of others." This did not mean that one had to hide one's light. Even Jesus "was not silent, he did show his wisdom." Jesus was, however, far from an attitude found in the seminary where, "One insults a colleague by saying: What do you know? You know nothing!....It is hard to imagine how much this can hurt someone." To live the love of Jesus means, of course, more: "He loved his enemies and asked for them—Father, please forgive them...."[30]

Stanggassinger took his students seriously, even in his sermons. He often spoke about obedience, but always about an enlightened obedience, never about blind obedience: "Do not obey just to appease authority because you are being threatened, or because you fear punishment! Obey out of love, obey from the heart. Then your obedience pleases God.... Let us be far from a police camp, where everything is done with reluctance, and only because there had been an order to do it....God does not want from us that which is forced upon us vehemently. He wants what we do freely, because we choose to do it out of love for him."[31] It is in this context that we should consider his admonition: "Of course, the walls of the juvenate protect you. But you are thinking, willing, decision-making, acting individuals, and not a mechanical construct. You yourselves must cooperate, and help...."[32]

There is one more thing to mention here: Stanggassinger put himself completely into his teaching and into his sermons: "You are the subject of my concern!" he told his listeners. He wanted to give them "all of his strength," he wanted to "serve" them.[33] In his notes, we can even find a sentence that one has to be ready to sacrifice oneself for the people with whom one has been entrusted, be ready even to die for them.[34] Therefore, these are not empty words: "You see, my dear students, we have received you from the hands of your fathers and mothers. Fatherly and motherly responsibility lies with us. A load that often weighs heavily upon my heart."[35] Because of this, he asked them for a small gift in return: their prayer, their "tuition," as he jokingly called it.[36]

There is a moving sentence in his final sermon: "Do not forget me, a poor sinner, so that I not may not be lost, while I am preaching to others. The highest gratitude you could show me is that you enthusiastically pray for me. Please spare me everything else."[37]

ENDNOTES

1 Causa Mon. 282.
2 Schriften III, passim.
3 Schriften III, 3, 20.
4 Zeugnisse 204.
5 Schriften III, 117–21.
6 Schriften III, 217.
7 Schriften III, 220f.
8 Schriften III, 222.
9 Schriften III, 149. Galatians 2:20.
10 Schriften III, 43 147, 230, 350.
11 Schriften III, 237.
12 Schriften III, 317.
13 Schriften III, 365.
14 Schriften III, 161.
15 Schriften III, 160.
16 Schriften III, 38.
17 Schriften III, 20ff.
18 Schriften III, 71.
19 Schriften III, 26.
20 Schriften III, 21.
21 Schriften III, 258.
22 Schriften III, 26.
23 Schriften III, 256.
24 Schriften III, 45, 76, 173.
25 Schriften III, 280, 286.
26 Schriften III, 52.
27 Schriften III, 54f., 59.
28 Schriften III, 49.
29 Schriften III, 228.
30 Schriften III, 388f., 390f.
31 Schriften III, 259f.
32 Schriften III, 199.
33 Schriften III, 38.
34 Schriften III, 185.
35 Schriften III, 290.
36 Schriften III, 107.
37 Schriften III, 351.

CHAPTER TEN

MUCH WORK AND EFFORT

"If one preaches in a scholarly way,
people say he is intelligent:
If one preaches in a way everyone can understand,
one can achieve something."

Before his ordination, Kaspar Stanggassinger pledged to go where he would be sent and to do what would be asked of him, to become everything to all people. He had to keep his promise. Many tasks were added to his job as teacher and educator, and he worked on them constantly.

Among them was a task that did not match his natural inclination: to Stanggassinger was handed over the seminary's bookkeeping. He often had to work late into the night, especially when the director, Father Wildgruber, ordered him to find an error in his figures by the following morning. "I have to do penance for my not taking my mathematics course seriously in school," quipped the annoyed prefect.[1]

Another specialized task also cost him many hours of work into the night. During the imminent move of the juvenate from Dürrnberg to Bavaria, the curriculum had to be adjusted to conform to Bavarian law. Even the rules of the house had to be approved by the Bavarian government. It was clear that the current, monastic rules of the juvenate would not be approved by the Bavarian ministry. Hence, new rules had to be written *pro forma,* that is, "only to present them but not intending to put them into practice." This was the thinking of the older fathers.

First, the "new" rules were elaborated on by Fathers Stracke and Wildgruber in cooperation with the teachers of the juvenate. Stanggassinger was given the assignment of the final editing of both the new curriculum and the juvenate regulations. When was he supposed to do this (in addition to all his day-to-day work) if not during *the night*? When, at last, he delivered the revision, all in handwritten duplicate, they were rejected as still not conforming to Bavarian guidelines. Then someone got the idea of obtaining, as a model, the rules and curriculum of the Royal Seminary in Arnberg; these had already been accepted almost as submitted. Again, Stanggassinger was charged with producing this draft. Finally, there were no objections; approval was given on September 9, 1897.[2]

The constant work at night had taken its toll on Stanggassinger's health. He was in an exhausted daze in the summer and autumn of 1897 and thought he would soon die. However, it was not only the nighttime work that was affecting him. When the new version of the rules was produced, the conflict between the older fathers and their younger confreres at the school reached a peak. The younger teachers did not see the new rules as a mere formality, and they insisted on full compliance. These new regulations offered an opportunity finally to ban all the leftover, unnatural strictness in the juvenate, putting an end to the "monastery in miniature."

Stanggassinger was caught; he suffered from being squeezed between the two groups. A confrere who experienced all this firsthand wrote, "He was a reformer in the best sense of the word. He was able to wait until the right moment, and he achieved a lot of good this way." Stanggassinger especially supported the idea of those colleagues who wanted to allow the students to go home during their vacation time. He said:

> During their vacation the juvenists learn good manners, a sign of fine culture, something that is completely missing with our people here. We accept many students without any kind of vocation, who stay for years but do not really want to be here, yet they do not find a real opportunity to leave. If they are allowed to go home, then they will have an opportunity to decide. This would be better for them and for the juvenate....Furthermore, it is very difficult to watch over them sixty to eighty hours a week for the two whole months of their vacation, especially when the weather is bad. It is easy for a bad mood to set in.

Stanggassinger spoke from experience. He tried to explain to his students why they were not allowed to go home. He got some unfriendly replies, such as, "It is easy for you to talk. You only need to walk a few steps and you are home. And you get visitors all the time."[3]

The main concern of the young teachers was also fully

supported by Stanggassinger: they pleaded for improved methods of classroom instruction and better staff training in how to be good high school teachers. Father Provincial Schöpf did not want to hear of it. He was of the opinion that in order to educate good, popular missionaries, the current approach to teaching sufficed.

A ray of light appeared late in the summer of 1897 when Father Karl Dilgskron of the Roman Generalate visited and supported the younger priests' goals. Dilgskron had a long discussion with Stanggassinger. It appears that Stanggassinger asked him to remove him from his office. However, Dilgskron disagreed. On September 26, 1897, he wrote to Rome, "We must treat the juvenate with care, which is difficult at the moment since the provincial leadership shows little interest in it; we must change this if we want to advance. Father Stanggassinger's work is excellent. We must help and encourage him."[4]

Let us return now to Stanggassinger's special tasks. Fresh out of the seminary, he had been named prefect of the brothers and of the candidates for the brotherhood in the "upper house." These men later remembered their prefect fondly. One of them reported that he remembered that during his free time, Stanggassinger would sit and talk with them. This was highly unusual at the time when there was a strict separation between fathers and brothers. Whenever they were short on food in the "upper house," he said, "You don't have to give me anything, make sure there is enough for the others." Stanggassinger also had the task of preparing the candidates spiritually for the novitiate. The first spiritual retreat that he prepared for his juvenists consisted of a reworking of his previous spiritual conferences to the brothers.[5]

Stanggassinger's most important "side job" was the pastoral care of different groups.[6] He was confessor to many of his students. While he never refused anyone, he was convinced that a complete separation between daily life in the seminary and his pastoral leadership would have been a better arrangement. Whenever he heard confessions in the church, the lines were long. "He combined a healthy strictness with incomparable kindness," wrote his first biographer.[7] He preferred going into the confessional reserved for the hard of hearing.[8] However, once, when one of the women religious of the area asked him to become her confessor, he replied, "I am much too strict for you."[9]

Stanggassinger would have liked to concentrate entirely on preaching sermons. Since he had been given the task of an educator, he consoled himself, "To do my part in caring for, maintaining, and developing this calling to religious life and priesthood is better than converting the greatest sinners and to conduct the best missions."[10] Only three times was he allowed to participate in parish activities. These were the devotional hours held in the archdiocese of Munich and Freising, once in Engelsburg and twice in Inzell.[11] And yet fifty sermons of Stanggassinger have been preserved.[12] He preached in Dürrnberg, in neighboring Schellenberg, and a few times in his hometown of Berchtesgaden. He gave most of his sermons, however, in the chapel of the Castle of

Wiesbach, near Hallein. Count Esterhazy was fascinated by his sermons. One could see, he said, that the preacher had a spirituality that was genuine.[13] One of his confreres reports that Stanggassinger was generally assigned to preach what in German were called "corner sermons." This meant preaching on ordinary Sundays, rather than delivering the "prestigious" sermons of major feast days. Stanggassinger remarked, "I am pleased that I get the 'corner sermons.' The feast day sermons require much more responsibility."[14]

Stanggassinger intended to preach as simply as possible in order to be understood by everyone. "If one preaches in a scholarly way, people say, 'he is intelligent. He understands everything!' But one does not achieve anything. However, if one preaches in a way that everyone can understand, then one can achieve something." Stanggassinger was convinced, "My words will not have an effect unless the grace of God prunes them. Nothing is gained without the Holy Spirit." He was fond of saying, "I am only the instrument through which God speaks."[15]

Perhaps this attitude explains the effectiveness of Stanggassinger's sermons. Decades later people would still remember them. Reading these sermons today, one asks the question: Why did they have such impact? Yes, the sermons are well-prepared. Questions, answers, and exclamations liven up the presentation. Stanggassinger knew how to speak clearly, in graphic language, demonstrating what he said with examples. However, this alone does not explain the impact of his sermons. It must have been the convincing personality behind the words. This lent an impressive tone to his words so that his listeners "caught" the message. It was his personal empathy that led people to look inward and turn more to God.[16]

What stands out is that many of Stanggassinger's sermons spoke of the Virgin Mary. That certainly cannot be explained only by the fact that the area near Salzberg and Berchtesgaden, with its many Marian chapels and pilgrimage sites, was truly "A Land of Mary." No doubt these "sanctuaries" provided many occasions for such sermons. But throughout his life Stanggassinger developed a deep, healthy veneration of the Mother of God. He had been brought up in the pilgrimage towns of Dürrnberg and Altötting, both dedicated to Mary. Moreover, he was convinced that she was still the caring Mother of all Christians. He had confidence that anyone who prayed to her would be led through life by her.

Yet, Stanggassinger's sermons are not exclusively focused on Mary. He often talked about the founder of his Congregation, Alphonsus Liguori. He communicated Alphonsus' central preoccupation: Christ becoming human, and Christ's redemption—and hence flows God's loving concern for the sinner, for which our response can be only one of love. Stanggassinger's first sermon combined both points: "Saint Alphonsus loved Mary; Mary loved Saint Alphonsus."[17]

Stanggassinger's pastoral work was largely restricted to sermons and confessions. This meant a difficult sacrifice for him, but he always understood his call to be an educator as a call to the "care of souls." His pastoral concern multiplied itself, as more than half of his students in turn became priests and Redemptorists. His pastoral enthusiasm and his love for neighbor formed them for life.

ENDNOTES

1 Causa Mon. 268; Zeugnisse 108.
2 Karl Kilgskron to Generalate, July 12, 1897, GAR P.G.S. VI B 3; PChr 145, 201; Untergehrer 24f., 40; *Meier* 151f.; Schuster–Wildenauer 111f.
3 *Meier* 152.; Causa Mon., 421; Zeugnisse 79; Juvenate Teachers to Generalate, July 5, 1900, GAR, P.G.S. VII A 2; Schuster–Wildenauer 117.
4 Karl Dilgskron to Generalate (see note 2); Visitation Report by Dilgskron, GAR, P.G.S., VI B 3; Dilgskron to Generalate, September 26, 1896, ibid.
5 Causa Mon. 350f., 374; Zeugnisse 202, 206.
6 Summarium 225.
7 *Meier* 168f.
8 Zeugnisse 91, 93.
9 *Meier* 169.
10 Schriften II/2, 136.
11 Schriften IV, 134; Zeugnisse 4.
12 Schriften IV, passim.
13 Countess Sophie von Esterhazy to Wildenauer, August 22, 1954, StAG.
14 Zeugnisse 200.
15 Causa Mon. 373; Zeugnisse 104.
16 Zeugnisse 93f; cf. Summarium 287f.
17 Schriften IV, passim.

CHAPTER ELEVEN

HIS LIFE IN GOD

*"Not wanting to do everything on one's own.
To let God do his work."*

Each week, teaching twenty-five hours in the school; every day monitoring the study room; always ready for a personal conversation with a student during leisure hours, either during recreation or on a walk; correcting homework until late in the night; preparing lessons and courses for the students who had to go through what was called the "one-year voluntary exam"[1]; keeping the financial books; lesson planning; copying the new seminary rules; lending a hand when desks, beds, and mattresses needed to be moved[2]; and, finally, the "short, apostolic excursions"—as he called them. There is no wonder that it all got to be too much for Stanggassinger. And we must ask, what happened to his "interior life?" Did he fall victim to superficial activism? Assuredly not!

The most surprising feature of this young priest, despite his varied work, despite his radical commitment, is that he remained, with all of his worries and concerns, a deeply religious man. He continued to grow deeper and deeper into his life-in-God, which was the center point of who he was and the mission he had.

The fact was that his tendency to act very methodically had an influence on his religious life. Many things that he worked hard to learn had become second nature to him. The fundamental explanation for this, of course, cannot be found in ascetical method or technique, but in his deep-rooted faith, in his readiness to be guided by grace and the Holy Spirit in his daily life.

Stanggassinger's spiritual notes of the time allow us to recognize two things. First, that only now did he subscribe to a clear, religious daily plan: "As a teacher and as prefect, I will visit the Blessed Sacrament daily at 7:30, at 10:00, and at 4:00. I will not get so absorbed in my daily work that my prayer life gets lost."[3] Second, his notes get simpler and simpler. It is not so much his own work that is placed in the foreground, but rather his complete devotion to God, and the guidance of God.

Stanggassinger wrote one year before his death, "Confidence in God's grace, mistrust about my own work, and worries. Not wanting to do everything on one's own. To let God work within me and, more than anything else, to look for paradise. The rest will follow." In another place he wrote, "Let us not strive for ideals we can never achieve, but let us fulfill day by day, hour by hour, as best we can the will of God." With a view to his multifaceted work, he observed, "If I live only for God I can use everything in the world to do good.... But be aware of any enterprise which is accompanied by too great a fervor, haste and lack of peace. And finally, "God alone is great. You put everything into the hands of your God. You harvest what you sow. All will grow for eternity."[4]

When reading such phrases, one comes to the conclusion that Stanggassinger, who had a healthy aversion toward false mysticism, private revelations, and extraordinary happenings, had found an inner peace amid the commotion and work of being teacher and prefect. He had arrived at his "center." Stanggassinger wrote down a paragraph from Saint John of the Cross, to which he added his own commentary at the end, which we note in italics:

> When one's soul has reached this state, then all of one's deeds, be they of a physical or a spiritual nature, all of one's work and all one's sufferings, serve to spread the love and the joy of God. Even one's life of prayer and interaction with God, that used to consist of meditation and exercises, has become simpler and has turned into this exercise of love. Thus, one, whether dealing with earthly or with spiritual things, can always say: "My only action is to continue in love.[5]—*This teacher of mysticism [Saint John of the Cross] adds that such a person is in a continuous state of a loving relationship with God, which begins with the alignment of his will with the will of God.*

Indeed God had become the center of Stanggassinger's life. Everything had its origin in that Divine Center, everything flowed into and was rooted in his "God Center." His everyday life, his work as an educator, his ministry as a pastor was fully found there. Stanggassinger knew, "The more love an apostolic worker possesses, the more fruitful his work."[6]

His prayer culminated there. "I want to exist as love, or I do not want to exist at all."[7]

Everything in his life came together in a life in God. We can only guess at the depth and intensity of this experience, glimpsing only fragments of his interior life. His colleagues noticed these fragments when they believed that Stanggassinger's daily action contained something surpassing all earthly greatness and achievements, even reaching into the power and the glory of God. Hesitantly and privately, because he had not done anything extraordinary, they called Stanggassinger a "saint." They saw in him a man in whom God's holiness appeared and became tangible.

Many said, "I want to become like him." "You have to follow him," a mother told her son when she saw Stanggassinger for the first time, "he is a saint."[8] And a former student noted, "When I came to Dürrnberg, I was disappointed that the Redemptorists did not look like real monks. Their garb was hardly any different from diocesan priests. That is, until I saw Father Stanggassinger for the first time...."[9]

Many who met him reported a similar experience. When urged to say more, they had difficulty in expressing exactly what impressed them so much. Whatever they did say about him does not reveal the secret of the man. "His exterior hinted at the deeply religious character of his soul," one witness claimed. "The way he celebrated Mass told of his living faith."

At his death it was discovered that he always carried an image of Our Mother of Perpetual Help on his chest.

His piety was free from strange peculiarities. Once, when he was in the chapel praying the Way of the Cross, some guests entered the chapel. He interrupted his prayer until the people had left. And yet, a confrere noticed tears running down his cheeks during the singing of the passion on Good Friday.

No one continued to wear items of clothing or shoes as long as he did. No one was as thrifty as he and took the vow of poverty as seriously as he did. An eager student wanted to clean his shoes. The suggestion was quickly refused. Stanggassinger cleaned his own shoes. At the table when there were only small portions, he quietly gave the server his portion to distribute to others. Only shortly before his death did he ask for a coat.[10]

These are moments in time, random observations. They are not much different from what people relate about other pious people. They are not absolutely what everybody does, yet the impression Stanggassinger made on others lingered on, and so they wanted to be like him.

"Many will be changed only through our example," Stanggassinger noted in September 1888.[11] His example had its effect. It did so precisely because the inner glow of his devotion to God did not show itself in extraordinary events, nor in exercises of virtue that were out of reach, nor in one-time, unrepeatable acts, but in his daily life, naturally. "In his exercise of virtue he never exceeded good measure," wrote one of the students. "That especially made us respect him. We thought, if he is a saint then we have a chance of getting to heaven."[12] And one of his biographers wrote, "He was one like any of us. He walked the same path that we walk, the path of the everyday fulfilling of our duties at work and in prayer. However, it is the way he walked this path—this is what made him a saint."[13]

ENDNOTES

1 Summarium 210.
2 Causa Mon., passim; Büche 53.
3 Schriften II/2, 112f.
4 Schriften II/2, 134f.
5 Johannes vom Kreuz (Saint John of the Cross) Collected Works in German), Vol. 4 Der geistliche Gesang (3rd ed. Munich 1957) 225.
6 Schriften II/2, 135.
7 Cf. "Vota Theologorum Censorum," Rome, March 18, 1958.
8 Causa Mon. 370: Summarium 255.
9 Zeugnisse 28.
10 Causa Mon., passim; Zeugnisse 105 and passim; Büche 54f.
11 Schriften II/2, 135.
12 Causa Mon. 357, 403; Summarium 179.
13 Büche 56.

CHAPTER TWELVE

FAITHFUL UNTIL DEATH

"Now my beloved, God has chosen me."

The Redemptorist Congregation had put great hopes in Stanggassinger. The Roman visitor Father Karl Dilgskron would have liked to see him as rector of a monastery in 1897. "Unfortunately," he stated, "he is still too young." A similar sentiment was expressed in the visitation report written by the provincial Father Matthias Baumgartner.[1] His successor, Father Aloysius Küppers, is said to have proposed Stanggassinger even for the office of provincial.[2] There was no doubt that after the juvenate had moved to Gars am Inn—the move planned for September 1899—Stanggassinger would be named director of the seminary.

What is more, on September 5, 1899, the provincial, Father Küppers, asked the superior general:

> Please allow me to propose Father Stanggassinger as superior for the fathers and brothers who live in the juvenate building. He is an exemplary Redemptorist, a diligent teacher, and he has been doing the financial accounting for the juvenate in Dürrnberg. He has also presented the Sunday spiritual conferences. I am convinced that he will fulfill the position to our satisfaction. In addition, he could be prefect for the professed students.[3]

However, things would turn out differently. Stanggassinger had not been feeling healthy for a while.[4] To regain his strength, his superiors pressured him during the summer vacations to eat an additional meal in the afternoon, which was unusual in the Congregation.[5] In contrast to their concern, however, is the workload that he was asked to carry. To all the tasks that he already had there was added the teaching of fourth-level high school German, Latin, and Greek—as well as religion classes for the five upper grades. This meant that he had accumulated a total of twenty-eight teaching hours per week. "He himself saw," one witness reports, "that he could not handle this in the long run." Therefore, one of his confreres advised him to ask the superiors to remove some of the load. But he said, "No, I will bear my cross until death."[6]

During August 1899, Stanggassinger often spoke of death.[7] He paid a farewell visit to Berchtesgaden and saw Sister Solana, the mother superior of the Mallersdorf Sisters, whose advice and prayers had accompanied him since childhood. Once more he prayed in the chapel in which he had served as an altar boy many times during his vacations.[8] When he bade farewell, he said, "This time it is final. I will not come here anymore. We will not meet again in this life."[9]

It did not seem possible that Stanggassinger was approaching the gates of eternity. One thought that nutritious food and physical activity would do him good. And there was plenty of opportunity for physical work during the vacation, since the move to Gars was imminent and furniture had to be transported. Stanggassinger joined in the work.

However, in addition to the work related to the move, he found time for five days of retreat. People say that he asked God to free him from his new tasks.[10] A short entry in his spiritual diary, however, shows that he had fully dedicated himself to his new responsibilities. He wanted to follow three principles: to develop his interior life more, despite all of the work; to observe the rules of the Congregation faithfully; and always to act mercifully toward his students.[11] Even the new fourth-level students, who until then had been taught at Bachham in Upper Bavaria and who did not yet know him, did not need to fear. "They do not have to be afraid of me," he wrote to the director in Bachham. "Even if, as a teacher, I do not take well to jokes, I still have the heart of a priest."[12]

On September 5, 1899, mathematics teacher Father Hubbauer and the soon-to-be ordained Sebastian Aigner traveled with twenty students of the Dürrnberg seminary to Gars. Barely a week later, on September 11, the seminary director, Father Aloysius Kraft and Stanggassinger followed, accompanied by another twenty-five students. They stood in front of the new and imposing seminary building, which had not been fully completed. The final plastering was still missing, the temporary barracks of the workers were still in the courtyard, and in the corridors workmen were still putting down tiles. On September 12, Stanggassinger furnished his room.[13] On the same day, Father Michael Siebler, who had gone to Brazil in 1894 and who had not seen Stanggassinger since then, arrived in Gars. Siebler reported, "When I met

Stanggassinger we greeted each other heartily. On the way to the juvenate, I told him, 'You will see, you will become director.' He replied in a serious tone, 'I will not. I asked God not to become a superior.' Laughing, I said, 'Then you will certainly become superior.' Then he looked at me with a stern expression, without saying a word. We parted in a happy manner without ever meeting again in this life."[14]

On September 13, 1899, the seminary in Gars was opened by celebrating Mass in the seminary chapel.[15] That same evening the juvenists' annual retreat began under Stanggassinger's direction. These days remained engraved in the memory of the participants. They were especially moved by the talk on death. Stanggassinger directed the thoughts of his juvenists to the deathbed of the young student Fischbach, whom most of them had known personally. "I know for sure that one of us will die in this house. If it may be one of you, or if it is I....I cannot say, only the good Lord knows." After the words "... if it is I...," he had remained quiet for a moment.

Was he weighing his words or did he pause because he sensed that he would die soon? His audience also remembered for a long time that he made the prayer of consecration at the end of the retreat with unusual devotion.[16]

Stanggassinger continued to talk about dying in the following days. For example, he did so at the start of the school year on September 18, 1899, when his confreres put pressure on him to reduce the number of hours at school. He told his juvenists, as if he wanted to apologize, "I am allowed to die. I have done enough for the Congregation."[17]

This is the last photo of Stanggassinger. It was taken a few weeks before his death in 1899.

This is the Redemptorist residence at Gars am Inn. In the foreground is the seminary, built in 1898–1899, in which Stanggassinger served as the first Prefect of Students.

A few days later he met Father Baudenbacher in the monastery gardens. Baudenbacher reports, "We went to the fathers' crypt and prayed there. I was soon finished with my prayer and moved on. When I turned around, Father Stanggassinger was still standing in front of the crypt. His face seemed transfigured. I went back and asked him which of the dead fathers he had loved the most. 'Father Baumgartner,' he replied." Did he know that he would soon rest beside him?[18]

On the same day the prefect arrived tired, even exhausted, at evening recreation. He had to sit down[19] and soon, as always, his students gathered around him. "Maybe I will soon be freed from my office," he said. "Like Father Baumgartner," replied one of the students. Stanggassinger may have been surprised and may have thought: Yes, like Father Baumgartner. The student continued, "He was relieved of his duties as rector in order to become provincial." Stanggassinger understood what he meant. "You want me to become director. This is only because I was never strict enough."[20] He felt a sense of relief when he was able to go off to his room. He was cold. Did he catch a cold in the new, damp building?

During the night of September 22–23, Stanggassinger's body began to ache. He got up and knocked at the room next to his, asking his neighbor to call Brother Joseph, who was the infirmarian of the house. It was shortly after midnight. When Brother Joseph entered his room, Stanggassinger apologized. He was sorry that he had to awaken him. He was sure that he had a hernia from all the lifting, packing, and unpacking.

If the infirmarian could just examine him, he could tell him whether it was just a hernia.

However, what happened afterward may have made the illness worse. He prescribed wet packs to relieve the pain. The next day Stanggassinger felt noticeably better. However, a doctor was called who diagnosed appendicitis but thought the patient would be well again soon.

During the day on Saturday, September 23, Stanggassinger did not get out of bed. He told a visitor at his bedside, "I always preach patience and devotion to God's will. Now the dear Lord has selected me and says, 'I would like to see how patient you are when I send you a cross to bear.' And I see that there is a big difference between preaching and suffering patiently."[21]

Much of his treatment can be explained only by the medicine of that era. Although it was later claimed that the doctors should have operated on him immediately, we cannot hold the doctors of the time responsible. The year 1899 was when the first appendix operations took place. Before 1899, they were impossible. At the time, castor oil and opium, enemas and mainly wet packs were usually prescribed. Today these remedies do not seem to make sense, and even seem harmful. In those days they constituted the usual therapy. Moreover, some of his contemporaries came to doubt if appendicitis was the correct diagnosis.[22] Several of the symptoms did not seem to match what was diagnosed, so even a malignant intestinal disease cannot be ruled out.

He was able to sleep through the night of September

23–24. Sunday morning he felt rested. He celebrated Mass in the heated chapel of the infirmary, and it would be his last. Thereafter, he showed a good appetite as he ate breakfast. When the infirmarian sat next to him and asked how he felt, he replied that he experienced some pain during Mass, but Christ on the cross certainly suffered more. Then he discussed with a brother the "dignity of the priesthood, the sacrament of penance, and the power of the priesthood." "I was surprised," this brother wrote, "that he spent so much time with me in conversation," since it was unusual and the rules of the Congregation did not allow that the fathers have long conversations with the brothers. The infirmarian was even more astonished when Stanggassinger told him the difficulties he had known in the novitiate and that his fellow novices had not helped the situation. But all that meant nothing when he thought of the joy of being a Redemptorist.

Suddenly the patient interrupted the conversation. Smiling, yet with firm voice he told the brother, "My dear friend, Brother Joseph, the best thing you can do now is to have someone give me the last rites."

The infirmarian grew alarmed, but he tried not to show it and said, "But Father Stanggassinger, one does not make a joke about this. Your Reverence just celebrated Mass, and here is the empty coffee cup. Death should be the farthest thing from your mind."

Stanggassinger looked intently at him and said, again with a smile, "Yes, yes, my dear brother, I will die quicker than all of you think."

The brother thought it wise to put Stanggassinger to bed. Soon it became obvious that his illness had not been overcome. Around eleven, he threw up, not being able to keep down any medicine.

When Brother Joseph looked in on his patient around three in the afternoon, the situation had become critical. The priest's entire body had become bloated, and the brother was justified in fearing the worst. The doctor, however, was of a different opinion. He said to continue the treatment, but this brought no relief.

On Monday morning, the patient suffered terrible pain. Now the doctor recognized the seriousness of the situation. The provincial quickly called for a second physician, a Doctor Bernhuber from Altötting. Both doctors then came to the same diagnosis: an inflammation of the peritoneum and an intestinal obstruction. It was clear to them that now any remedy was impossible. However, Father Kraft, who toward evening was called on to administer the last rites, was of a different mind. "It cannot be dangerous," he said, "our good God knows we still need him."[23]

Two seminarians who served as sacristans in the juvenate were called to prepare the room for the last rites. They were frightened as they saw their prefect, who seemed to stammer nonsense. He called the two of them to his bed and said, "Do you remember how a good student dies?" He was hinting at his talk on the "death of a good person" from the recent retreat. "I did not have the impression," one of the two students wrote later, "that he wanted to say, 'Look, I am a good person.' Rather he tried to say, 'Even I still have to learn how to die. When it comes to dying, I am still a student!' Then Stanggassinger added, 'I am not afraid of dying.' Finally he urged them to stay true to their vocation. When he wanted to continue, the infirmarian asked him to spare himself. Then he blessed both of them."[24]

With tears in their eyes, the two who had served as acolytes left the room. When they arrived at the dormitory all the students were still awake. "How is he?" the two were asked. After their report many of the students got up to pray the rosary while others waited at night in front of the room of their ill prefect.[25]

Around eleven he fell asleep, and near one in the morning, he started to talk in his sleep. It seemed as if he wanted to preach. "Dear juvenists," he started, "praise and love the Mother of God. Visit Jesus in the tabernacle at the altar. He lives with us under the same roof. You may tell him everything that bothers you. Talk to him as a child talks to his father!" Then he said, "Many pious people are afraid of the devil. They should be afraid of something else: bad people."

Doctor Bernhuber approached the bed. "You are a good doctor," Stanggassinger said. Then he continued with his sermon. Suddenly he sat upright in bed and asked for holy Communion, which was given to him. The patient prayed aloud the prayers of preparation for holy Communion and then the prayers of thanksgiving as written by Saint Alphonsus. He knew them by heart.

The infirmarian reported, "His voice became softer and

softer, while saying other brief prayers. His took breaths that grew shorter and more deliberate. There was cold sweat on his forehead. We could no longer find a pulse."

At 3:45 on Tuesday morning, September 26, 1899, Father Kaspar Stanggassinger died.[26]

Soon thereafter, at this unusual time, the juvenists were awakened. "Father Stanggassinger is dead!" Sobbing could be heard in their dormitory.[27]

ENDNOTES

1 Visitation Reports, GAR, P.G.S. VI.
2 Zeugnisse, 206.
3 Küppers to Generalate, September 9, 1899, GAR, P.G.S., V A 3.
4 Cf. Causa Mon.. 421; Schriften II/2, 126ff.
5 Schuster–Wildenauer 136f.; *Meier* 214f.
6 *Meier* 257f.
7 Cf. Causa Mon., 386.
8 Causa Mon. 172, 217; Zeugnisse 111, 142f.
9 Zeugnisse 111; *Meier* 250.
10 Causa Mon. 149.
11 Schriften II/2, 136.
12 Schriften V, 132.
13 Untergehrer 59f; PChr 249f.
14 *Meier* 254.
15 PChr 250.
16 Zeugnisse 26; Causa Mon 284, 387.
17 *Meier* 257f.
18 Zeugnisse 205.
19 Summarium 218.
20 *Meier* 259.
21 Zeugnisse 97.
22 Causa Mon. 351, 357; Summarium 227.
23 Zeugnisse 97ff.
24 Zeugnisse 80f.; Suppl. 13; Summarium 227.
25 Causa Mon. 413.
26 Zeugnisse 99ff.
27 Zeugnisse 81.

CHAPTER THIRTEEN

A SHINING LIGHT

"When I heard of his death,
I immediately asked for his intercession."

FRANCIS XAVIER PLEITHNER

Father Stanggassinger's death was an incredible blow to his students and to his confreres. The director of the Bachham seminary, Father Joseph Atzberger—who would later assume Stanggassinger's position in Gars—wrote in his diary, "An irreplaceable pillar of the juvenate has crumbled." Similar was the reaction on the part of Stanggassinger's colleague and first biographer, Father Alois Meier. On the morning of September 26, 1899, when he entered the room in which the deceased Redemptorist lay, he sobbed loudly. He went over to his body and pressed his hand firmly. Others followed his example.[1]

Around ten o'clock the body was laid out in the monastery and the seminarians said their final goodbyes to their prefect. One student at the bier, Karl Härle, spoke aloud, "I liked him so much. Now he is dead. How quickly one can go away from us."[2]

Only two days after he died, Stanggassinger was buried. The juvenists sang the *Miserere* by Palestrina, and the provincial, Father Aloysius Küppers, for his funeral homily chose the theme based on a paraphrase of Wisdom 4:13, "Although dying young, a good and just man has nevertheless had a full life."[3]

Immediately after the burial, Father Küppers wrote to Rome, since he had to respond to the letter he had received about new appointments in the province. Concerning Stanggassinger, Rome had gladly accepted the provincial's suggestions. Stanggassinger had been named director and superior of the fathers and brothers of the juvenate. He should have written a thank-you letter. However, now the letter had to say:

> Last Sunday evening I received the list of new appointments. At that time Father Stanggassinger was deathly ill with appendicitis. Despite diligent care and the attentive treatment of two doctors we could not save this precious life. The capable physician from Altötting, Doctor Bernhuber, whom I telegraphed to come, spent most of the night from Monday to Tuesday at his patient's bed. Alas, in vain. The same night around 3:30 a.m. our dear confrere died in an edifying manner. The infirmarian, Brother Joseph, said he had never seen a confrere die in such an edifying way. It was a beautiful experience for him to assist the dying man.[4]

Many people expressed their condolences to Stanggassinger's family and to the Redemptorists at Gars. In their letters they combined sadness with certainty that the departed was with God. Thus, a classmate of Stanggassinger in Freising and now a professor in Echstätt, Ludwig Eisenhofer, wrote to the mother of the deceased, "As long as I had contact with him, I enjoyed his solidly devout personality, his striving to live with an orientation toward God above. I am obliged openly to confirm that your son lived as an ideal priest. Now his life has been crowned by the death of a saint."[5]

Stanggassinger's former director of the minor seminary wrote, "He must have died well. We die the way we live. In him I hope to have an intercessor."[6] And his confessor in Freising for many years, Professor Francis Xavier Pleithner: "When I heard of his death, I prayed, of course, for the deceased, but with the thought that if he did not need our prayers, I immediately asked for his intercession. In my first sorrow, in which I asked him for help, God directed everything well beyond what I had not ever dared to hope. Since then I have confidently called on his help a number of times."[7]

The members of the Redemptorist Congregation reacted in a reserved manner, although Father John B. Frankenberger reportedly said, "Stanggassinger was my best novice," and furthermore, "Stanggassinger is a saint in the full meaning of the word." Nevertheless, it seemed impossible for most of them that Stanggassinger was a "saint."[8] Father Meier had collected reports about his former colleague's high school years and sent them to the province headquarters; then he also came to the conclusion that Stanggassinger had to be rescued from oblivion. But even Meier thought of him as "a good religious and priest, not as a saint."[9]

"What ruckus are people causing because of him?" commented Father Caspar Stamm, known as "The Godfather" of the Southern German Redemptorists. When timidly asked by a young priest whether anyone should begin the process of canonization, Father Aloysius Kraft, the last director of the juvenate at Dürrnberg answered, "That is too much!" Even the provincial, Father Küppers, who had placed his hopes in Father Stanggassinger, admitted to a young priest that he did not know what to say at the grave. But he asked this father to jot down a few points about Stanggassinger's life.[10]

All of this is reminiscent of another saint, despite the differences in gender and in her particular path to God. She had two things in common with Stanggassinger. Her biographical data is almost the same as Stanggassinger's, for she was born in 1873 and died in 1897. Like Stanggassinger, she walked the path of everyday faithfulness. We refer here to Thérèse of Lisieux. Her sisters in religious life said at her death: "What will our mother superior be able to write in her eulogy?"[11]

The memory of the revered Stanggassinger lived on. This was not due to an autobiography, as happened with the Carmelite saint of Lisieux. It was not even due to the first biography done by Father Alois Meier and published in 1902. Kaspar Stanggassinger had etched himself into the many hearts of his classmates and other students in Freising, and especially into the hearts of his students in Dürrnberg. The older they got and the more life experience they gathered, the clearer it became to them what an extraordinary man Stanggassinger had been. A priest who studied with him in Freising and who followed him to the Redemptorist monastery described him toward the end of his life as follows: "Father Stanggassinger was a saint. While we do not know of any extraordinary great deeds, obvious mortification, miracles, or mystical qualities, it is nonetheless heroic how he served God from his childhood until his death. I cannot remember meeting a similar holy priest and religious man in my life as a priest."[12]

Similar testimonies abound. They keep mentioning that there was a young man who did nothing extraordinary but what the day demanded. They said something in him shone forth and those who met him could not forget it—it was something of the love of God, something of the goodness of God. It is here that we can look for the secret of his holiness. The result was that it seemed natural for many of his students and confreres to pray to him for help.

In January 1934 there was a meeting of the superiors of the Munich province. Almost all the participants had been Stanggassinger's students. It seemed natural, then, that in this meeting, one of the fathers began what had been neglected at the start of the century: the beatification process of Kaspar Stanggassinger.[13]

On January 9, 1935, his body was moved from the crypt of the monastery in Gars to the chapel of the Sacred Heart of Jesus. The archbishop of Munich and Freising, Michael Cardinal von Faulhaber, attended the ceremony and delivered the sermon. Without preempting the verdict of the Church, he described Stanggassinger as a "shining light" for the archdiocese, the Redemptorist Congregation, for students, and for all Catholic people.[14]

The next step began on April 8, 1935, in Munich; this

was the required episcopal process of gathering information. On that day, Father Francis Abele handed over the reports and the *positio,* which is the statement indicating the holiness of Stanggassinger's life. A great number of witnesses were interviewed in Germany and in Brazil. (Many of Stanggassinger's fellow students were then in the Brazilian mission). On June 10, 1936, the interviews ended.[15]

At this point, all of Stanggassinger's written notes had to be examined. The task was completed on July 24, 1942. The episcopal process finished on April 14, 1959. It included a summary of the testimonies, a report on the life and virtues of "the Servant of God," and also any objections along with their rebuttal.

On April 26, 1960, the apostolic process was opened in Rome. This was the second phase toward beatification. After the initial approval by the responsible Vatican commission, then the bishop's documents were presented for a kind of reevaluation. Once again, witnesses were interviewed, the casket was opened, examined, and sealed. On February 14, 1964, Cardinal Döpfner finalized this process of reacceptance. Again, a summary of all the testimonies was printed. Then it was the turn of the Roman theologians. Objections were raised and refuted. In 1979, the entire documentation was handed over to the Roman Congregation for the Causes of Saints. On January 16, 1986, the decree was published that confirmed that Stanggassinger had exercised the theological virtues of faith, hope, and love, and the cardinal virtues of prudence, temperance, fortitude, and justice, as well as all the other virtues in a heroic manner. All obstacles for beatification had been cleared, provided there was a miracle. The miracle was confirmed by doctors on January 7, 1987.

Maria Theophilus Kleeburg of the Sisters of Niederbron had undergone two stomach operations without much success. Another operation was required, and when this surgery was in process it had to be interrupted because of a weak heart. The sister was sent to the motherhouse and was considered terminal. On April 6, 1935, she, along with some of the other sisters began a novena in their convent in honor of Father Stanggassinger. On April 8, 1935 (the day on which his beatification process began), the sister was free from all pain. The doctors who heard about it were at first unconvinced. However, Sister Maria Theophilus remained healthy from then on, was able to eat what she wanted, and could accomplish all of her work. The doctors confirmed, "This is the work of a higher power." She died in March 1957 at the age of seventy.

In June 1987, a commission of theologians gathered in Rome. They confirmed the doctor's certificate, dated January 7 of the same year. On October 20, 1987, a commission of cardinals recognized the miracle. At this point only papal approval was needed, and this was promulgated by the decree of December 11, 1987. In Rome on April 24, 1988, Father Kaspar Stanggassinger was declared Blessed.[16]

ENDNOTES

1 Diary, StAG; Zeugnisse 207; *Meier* 269.
2 Summarium 219.
3 Summarium 219; cf Causa Mon. 354, 382.
4 Küppers to Generalate, September 29, 1899, GAR, P.G.S. V A 3.
5 Zeugnisse 5.
6 Zeugnisse 1.
7 Zeugnisse 31.
8 Causa Mon. 331, 391.
9 Summarium 234.
10 Zeugnisse 208.
11 I.F. Görres, *Die "kleine" Thérèse, Das Senfkorn von Lisieux* (Freiburg 1964) 9.
12 Causa Mon. 391.
13 Summarium 260; Schuster–Wildenauer 149f.
14 Cardinal Faulhaber about Stanggassinger, Gars am Inn (n.d.).
15 Causa Mon., passim.
16 Schuster–Wildenauer 152f.; various documents and opinions relating to Beatification, StAG.

CHAPTER FOURTEEN

A SAINT FOR TODAY

"His amiable nature, full of unusual charity, constitutes a model for our time."

The veneration of saints has become suspect. One finds people who think, why the hero-worship? Is this not outdated? Would it not be better to put the time and money into charitable enterprises instead of the process of beatification? Furthermore, who generally become beatified? Is it not religious priests and brothers and sisters—because they have an influential lobby wanting to populate heaven with many of their stars?

We may ask these skeptical, even critical, questions. Questions that do seem reasonable, human, and even Christian.

Kaspar Stanggassinger would probably be the last to disagree with these concerns. He is supposed to have said that it would be best to be beatified only on Judgment Day. That would not cost anything.[1]

However, there are also other views. When the pope declares a person a saint, he wants to state that here is someone who was an example of a Christian life based on God. This does not refer only to so-called "great" saints with an important place in history. But it also applies to the so-called "little" saints who may go unnoticed by historians. Not everyone has the talent and the opportunity to renew the global church as did the charismatic Francis of Assisi. Not everyone has the oratorical gifts of Bernard of Clairvaux. Or the wisdom of Augustine of Hippo. Or the intellectual acuteness of Thomas Aquinas. Not everyone is called to challenge emperors, dictators, and other rulers. Not everyone can live among lepers on an island.

But anyone can "*Do What the Day Demands*" in the place where God has placed her or him, and do it with love.

Anyone can be there for the people who need them day in and day out. So this is the meaning of a "little saint," a saint for everyday life, whose life is just as important before God as that of the "great ones" with their extraordinary deeds. We know their environment. We know their obligations. It is here that we see Father Kaspar Stanggassinger's importance.

In him we find a man who did not reach even the age of twenty-nine. He did not achieve anything outstanding, anything about which the history books will report, anything which could somehow be the basis for a play or a film. He founded no religious Congregation. He was not a resistance fighter, or a great theologian, or one who sought the limelight. He was a simple minor seminary prefect who was loved by his students. He was never controversial because, as they say, he was "too good."[2] When his career had just started, he died. The illness leading to his death was nothing extraordinary. Not long afterward a relatively minor surgery was developed that perhaps would have saved him.

Of course, the Roman theologians who had to judge Kaspar Stanggassinger's holiness noted all these things. In their written opinions, they allude to all this. "Extraordinary events," they say, "are missing from Stanggassinger's life. Only two episodes stand out from the everyday life, the mountain rescue of a friend, and the unusual fortitude in facing his father, who wanted to dissuade him from his vocation. Nothing else of special importance is mentioned in the testimonies."[3]

Hence the theologians asked themselves: "Is this only a great priest, a diligent religious man, or a genuine saint, a man whose life may serve as an example for other faithful?" They reached the verdict, "Holiness does not consist of external events. It is essentially a richness of grace and a God-centered life. Such richness in daily life can be manifest in an unusual way, not through spectacular deeds, but by a constant faithfulness that grows out of never-ending love."[4]

There is no doubt: Stanggassinger led a holy life. How does his life become an example for our everyday lives? We can see how—when we trace out the path of his life's journey.

First, there was his deep faith. For him, God was close by. For Stanggassinger, God was his true reality. And it was the God who became human and who redeemed the human family on the cross. This was for him a God who deserves all of our love. "God is everything, I am nothing."

Secondly, there was his steady pursuit of his faith: what was important was to love God with all one's strength, with ultimate commitment (see Luke 10:27). What mattered was to become holy. He saw that this is something impossible without self-knowledge and hard work on oneself. One was not to be distracted in following Christ to God. But there could be no haste, just as in hiking in the mountains, putting "one step after another."

Now, add to this his knowledge that human actions have no value if the Holy Spirit does not inspire them. Grace is everything.

Furthermore, the secular world was to be taken seriously. Love of nature affected his holiness. For example, witness his love of the mountains. In a lecture shortly before his death, Stanggassinger stated that he felt a kinship to Jesus in the mountains. Stanggassinger also loved his home and his family. To the amazement of his confreres, he was in close contact with his family, even when he was at the monastery. The death of a family member struck at his heart. Care for his students "made his heart heavy," as he wrote in his last letter.[5] This is "human" wisdom and maturity necessary even for Christians.

We also recognize his healthy skepticism of all exaggeration and abnormality in religious life, his contentment with "little things," and with "what the day demands."

Specifically, his holiness expressed itself in steadfast friendliness, charity, a readiness to help, respect for his fellows and their opinions, and putting himself second, with humility. So the documents of his beatification underline: "His amiable nature, full of unusual charity, composes a model for today's youth."

Finally, there is Stanggassinger's life as an educator. For him, education mainly meant pastoral care. He saw his task as leading closer to Christ all the young people entrusted into his care. Leisure, studies, his own physical well-being—in fact, everything—was secondary to this goal. And yet his students were always more than simply objects of education and pastoral care. He always tried to convince, not to force. He knew full well that his students were independent persons. He did not want to order them. He wanted to inspire them.

Here is the relevance of this young Christian man. He is not a hero we cannot get in touch with, and whose "unreachable" life may not even be worth imitating.

Heinrich Böll once wrote about such impossible heroes, saying that "they use time and everything in it recklessly. They risk their own lives and the lives of everyone whom history places in their path. They must be eliminated."[6]

Stanggassinger's life was ordinary. He did what many can do and, indeed, have done. Since the center of his life was God, he did not live in vain. His life can inspire us to succeed in our own life as well.

ENDNOTES

1 Zeugnisse 22.
2 J. Zartmann to Generalate, December 21, 1898, GAR, P.G.S. VII A 1.
3 *Relatio et Vota congressus peculiaris super virutibus* (Rome 1985) 45f.
4 Ibid., 74.
5 Schriften V, 126.
6 L. Kopelew, *Der heilige Doktor Fjodor Petrowitsch. Die Geschichte des Friedrich Josef Haas* (Hamburg 1984), preface, 9.

SOURCES

Generally it is not usual procedure to provide footnotes to a popular biography. However, we have chosen to differ from that norm at the expressed wish of the current confreres of this new Redemptorist Blessed. Our intent is to make clear that nothing in this book is pious legend. Each statement can be verified.

The sources are perfectly accessible. Everything Stanggassinger wrote during his lifetime has been preserved, at least in copy-form or transcript. This includes his personal spiritual notes, sermons, letters, and speeches. Letters to him and about him, and all official documentation complete these primary sources.

In addition, there are the very detailed testimonials concerning his life. These can be grouped into three parts. First, there are detailed reports from 1899 until 1902. They were collected at the urging of Stanggassinger's first biographer and served as a source for that first biography. These reports are valuable because of their immediacy. It is the aim of the reports to preserve the memory of a valued teacher, confrere, and friend, but not to portray him as a saint. Thus some things are recorded that do not fit the image of a saint, and these would later prove especially valuable.

The second part of the testimonials come from the process for beatification. The witnesses' testimonies were collected in the episcopal process in Munich from 1935 to 1937. They were completed by the letters of the vice postulator, Father Francis Abele. Some of these reports are of little value. There is an undeniable tendency to fit Stanggassinger into one's own limited view of sainthood. Yet we also find some sober and critical reports. Some witnesses see it as their duty to correct one-sided and cookie-cutter-like descriptions of holiness.

Finally, on the occasion of the process conducted by the Holy See in the 1960s, some witnesses who had not yet been heard were then questioned. These were mainly Stanggassinger's students. They were able to add some details.

As for the biographies produced to date, they also serve as sources. This is especially true for the first biography, that of Father Alois Meier. Meier lived with and knew Stanggassinger personally. He was outstanding in his ability to produce a critical historical work. Therefore, his descriptions are exceptionally credible. This cannot be said of the fanciful writer Father Joseph Schuster. Yet, as one of Stanggassinger's former students, he, too, could attest to what he saw and heard. The least valuable source was the well-written biography by Father Kurtdietrich Büche. A few details, which can be found only in Büche's book, are probably based on witnesses, but Büche did not know Stanggassinger.

In our biography we tried to let primary sources and witnesses speak whenever possible. The published literature was consulted only in cases where they could be clearly considered as primary sources and other documents were unavailable, or where they provide additional information that was unavailable elsewhere.

EXPLANATIONS OF ENDNOTES ABBREVIATIONS

Büche: Büche, Kurtdietrich. *P. Kaspar Stanggassinger, Redemptorist* (Meitingen 1939; Traunreut, third edition, 1982).

Causa Mon.: *Causa Monacensis Beatificationis Servi Dei Gaspari Stanggassinger sac. Prof. CSsR Processus informativus super fama sanctitatis vitae, virtutum et miraculorum in genere, anno Domini, 1935–1936*. This is the investigation into the holiness of the life of Stanggassinger, which was conducted in Munich; the original typewritten document is in the Redemptorist archives at Gars.

Commentarii: *Commentarii de Rebus in Provincia Germaniae Superioris gestis [annis] 1901–1912* (Ratisbonae et Cambi [Regensburg and Cham]) 1903 onward. In Latin, these are printed chronicles of events in the Upper German CSsR Province. Volumes are relatively rare; copy in GAR.

GAR: Generalate Archives of the Redemptorists, Rome (especially correspondence between the Provincial of the Upper German Province and the Superior General in Rome).

Mayer: Mayer, Anton. *Die Errichtung des Lyzeums in Freising im Jahre 1834. Eine Studie zu Kulturgeschichte des Restaurationszeitalters. Festgabe zur Feier des 100 jährigen Bestehens des Philos.-theol. Hochschule Freising,* Munich and Freising 1934. This volume deals with historical and cultural aspects of the Freising Philosophical-Theological University since its founding in 1834.

Meier: Meier, Alois. *P. Kaspar Stanggassinger. Ein würdiger Sohn des heilingen Alfons M. Von Liguori* (Mühlsdorf 1902; Cham, 2nd ed., 1908 (references are to the 2nd ed.) The first biography of Stanggassinger; subtitle means "A worthy son of Saint Alphonsus Liguori."

Meier: Meier, Alois, Karl Bauden et al. *Lebensbilder verstorbener Redemptoristen* (typescript). These are biographies of deceased Redemptorists, PAG.

PAG: Provincial Archives at Gars, especially personnel files.

PChr: *Provinzchronik, 1892–1900,* handwritten province chronicles, found in PAG.

Schriften: *Schriften Stanggassingers.* Five volumes of writings by Stanggassinger, mainly transcriptions of the shorthand originals. Found in StAG.

Schuster-Wildenauer: Schuster, Josef. *Der Diener Gottes P. Kaspar Stanggassinger, Redemptorist 1871–1899, Ein Leben für die Jugend,* Munich, 1937; 2nd ed. by Karl Wildenauer, Gars, 1960. Title translation: *The Servant of God, Father Kaspar Stanggassinger, Redemptorist, 1871-1899, A Life for Young People.*

Six: Six, Anton. *Zum goldenen Jubiläum der Marianischen Studentkongregation in Freising am 8 Dezember 1911,* Freising 1911. Title translation: *For the Golden Jubilee of the Marian Student Society in Freising, December 8, 1911.*

StAG: Stanggassinger Archives at Gars am Inn.

Summarium: *Beatificationis et Canonizationis servi Dei Gasparis Stanggassinger sac. Prof congr. SS. Red, (+1899). Summarium super dubio: An constet de virtutibus...in casu ad effectum de quo agitur, Monacen. et Frisingen,* Rome 1973. This is a summary of later investigations held at Munich and Freising as part of the investigation into the virtuous life of Stanggassinger, looking toward his possible Beatification and even Canonization. Printed in Rome in 1973.

Untergehrer: Untergehrer, J. *Studentatschronik,* vol. II. Chronicles of events in the studendate. Found in StAG.

Weiss: Weiss, Otto. *Die Redemptoristen in Bayern (1790–1909), Ein Betrag zur Geschichte des Ultramontanismus,* Saint Ottilien 1983. Title translation: *The Redemptorists in Bavaria (1790-1909), a Contribution to the History of Ultramontanism.*

Zeugnisse: Zeugnisse, "Klemmbinder III," the third "clamp-binder" containing letters and reports of Stanggassinger's life, 1899-1902, with reports from 1935 onward. Found in StAG. These were especially useful reports, some of which have been incorporated into official documentation.